ENGAGING, MOTIVATING AND EMPOWERING

LEARNERS IN SCHOOLS

ENGAGING, MOTIVATING AND EMPOWERING

LEARNERS IN SCHOOLS

DES HEWITT & BRITTANY WRIGHT

Los Angeles | London | New Delhi
Singapore | Washington DC | Melbourne

Los Angeles | London | New Delhi
Singapore | Washington DC | Melbourne

SAGE Publications Ltd
1 Oliver's Yard
55 City Road
London EC1Y 1SP

SAGE Publications Inc.
2455 Teller Road
Thousand Oaks, California 91320

SAGE Publications India Pvt Ltd
B 1/I 1 Mohan Cooperative Industrial Area
Mathura Road
New Delhi 110 044

SAGE Publications Asia-Pacific Pte Ltd
3 Church Street
#10-04 Samsung Hub
Singapore 049483

Publisher: James Clark
Editorial assistant: Diana Alves
Production editor: Nicola Carrier
Proofreader: Leigh C. Smithson
Indexer: Gary Kirby
Marketing manager: Dilhara Attygalle
Cover design: Naomi Robinson
Typeset by: C&M Digitals (P) Ltd, Chennai, India
Printed in the UK

Library of Congress Control Number: 2018936824

British Library Cataloguing in Publication data

A catalogue record for this book is available from the
British Library

ISBN 978-1-4739-9504-8
ISBN 978-1-4739-9505-5 (pbk)

At SAGE we take sustainability seriously. Most of our products are printed in the UK using responsibly sourced
papers and boards. When we print overseas we ensure sustainable papers are used as measured by the PREPS
grading system. We undertake an annual audit to monitor our sustainability.

TABLE OF CONTENTS

ABOUT THE AUTHORS

As Head of Primary and Early Years Teacher Education at the University of Warwick, **Des Hewitt** places teaching and learning at the heart of his work. With over 25 years of teaching experience in schools and universities, he has been recognised for his national and international profile in Teacher Education. He was awarded a National Teaching Fellowship by the Higher Education Academy and is a Professorial Teaching Fellow at Warwick.

Des has experience of promoting and evolving the model of placements for trainee primary school teachers, in England and in other countries. He has also been involved in advising UK government organisations on developing English and reading for university Initial Teacher Training (ITT) providers. In addition, he has led universities in developing practice in special education needs and disability. He also sat on a steering group in the Department for Children, Schools and Families, evaluating the impact of training for inclusion in teacher education.

Working with schools and the Teacher Education sector in Tanzania has been a focus for Des in recent years. Collaborative projects with researchers and educators in Finland, Germany, India and Hungary have also provided the opportunity to share ideas about teacher education, partnership development and research skills, internationally. Des supports emerging researchers through the European Educational Research Association.

Publications include a focus on innovation, English as an Additional Language (EAL) and Effective Learning, mental health and mindfulness, matching his research interests. Recently, he has lead research evaluation of educational practice in the arts and agricultural sectors. He is a Director of several multi-academy trusts. Through these he is able to support school improvement and the development of a good education for children and professionals. Des is always committed to working in partnership with others.

Brittany Wright is a Teaching Fellow at the Centre for Teacher Education at the University of Warwick. She previously worked in secondary education. Although her most recent role was as Head of English in a large secondary school, Brittany has also led on provision for higher-ability learners and co-ordinated widening participation programmes focused on supporting learners from disadvantaged backgrounds in pursuing further and higher education. Since moving into initial teacher education, Brittany has also worked with schools in North London, supporting professional development of teachers, as well as teaching across Primary and Secondary PostGraduate Certificate in Education (PGCE) programmes.

1

INTRODUCTION TO ENGAGEMENT, MOTIVATION AND EMPOWERMENT

Chapter guide

In this chapter, you will learn about:

- Why this book, why now?

- Teachers and pupils: Why we need to consider the development of both together

- Key concepts: Engagement, motivation and empowerment

- Who would find this book relevant?

- Case study examples and how the chapters are organised

- Making the links to school-based training for teachers

- Overview of the chapters

Learning matters in society. It is the life force that flows through the past, the present and the future. Without a good education, we have no learning. Without learning, we have nothing.

We write this book as a positive statement to explain the concept of a good education and the role of engagement, motivation and empowerment. We believe in the rights and responsibilities of all learners to experience a good education. We make no apologies for emphasising democracy, agency and the right to flourish. These are the roots of this book.

Whilst learning can happen anywhere, it is principally in early years, primary and secondary settings that education in a more formal sense takes place. Of course, universities and professional settings also provide keystones in the education system. But here, our focus is on schools. Schools very much reflect society in terms of the value and characteristics of education.

We believe that a good education can only be achieved by engaging, motivating and empowering all learners in school. This way, everyone will flourish as individuals whilst making a positive contribution to society. Whilst there are individual, institutional and societal factors in both pupils and teachers that have an impact, the content structure and experience of education is critical. This book will examine the issues.

Why this book, why now?

A good education recognises different levels of learning in the classroom. This includes knowledge, skills and understanding. Moreover the development of social, emotional and, perhaps critically, core values are central to a good education. These are inextricably linked. Without knowledge and the skills to discuss the world, how can we generate strong values? Without strong values, how can we learn about the world in an ethical way, applying knowledge and working with others appropriately? Life is as much about doing the right thing as it is about doing things right. There is therefore no opposition between the development of strong core skills and strong core values. We cannot have a good education without developing the various aspects of learning – knowledge, skills, social, emotional and ethical learning – in both pupils and teachers. Both teachers and pupils deserve a good education.

Teachers and pupils: Why we need to consider the development of both together

Writing a book about learning is as much a process of self-discovery as articulating the current landscape of learning in schools. We hope that reading this book, however you do that, will facilitate your own journey of discovery. You will find in this book a review of current thinking around 'engagement, motivation and empowerment' of learners in school. By 'learners', we mean children and young people as learners, as well as teachers as learners. The central tenet of the book is the need to consider, in parallel, the development of both teachers and pupils. There is always an interaction between the lives of pupils and the lives of teachers in the classroom, at cognitive, social, emotional and moral levels. Bronfenbrenner's ecological theory of development captures the interaction between the learner and their environment (Bronfenbrenner, 1992). It recognises the interconnectedness of the teacher and the learner. It is useful to consider who is the learner and who is the teacher. It is not quite as simple as you would think. In the work of Loris Malaguzzi, the role of the teacher is to discover the way in which the very young child learns, to understand the 'hundred languages' of the child (Edwards et al., 1998). In a very special way, the teacher learns from the child and the child teaches the teacher. But even in more formal learning settings, there is always a sense that the teacher can only be effective if they pitch a lesson at the current level of the learner. This means knowing the learner.

We take this model further to consider this at the level of engagement, motivation and empowerment. These concepts are introduced and referenced to recent educational theories. What are the principles underlying successful development of both pupils and teachers, and how might parallel processes, needs and concerns manifest in the classroom? We explore these principles and practices with reference to relevant theory, exemplifying them with authentic case studies from primary and secondary schools. Teachers and pupils are inextricably linked. This is why we need to consider their learning as being linked, and why this book is about the learning of pupils and the learning of teachers. We have a particular commitment to teachers at the early stages of their career. How did we learn to be teachers? What can we do to support new and early career teachers? Likewise, we have a responsibility to ensure that the next generation of learners has a great experience in schools, invested with all the knowledge and attributes to become and lead the next stage in our society. Only great teachers with a good education can provide the context, leadership and passion needed for a good education in schools. If we do not engage, motivate and empower teachers, how can we possibly do the same for children and young people? Disaffected, demotivated and disempowered professionals do not make good teachers.

Key concepts: Engagement, motivation, empowerment, mutuality and agency

In this book, you will be introduced to different aspects of engagement, motivation and empowerment. Whilst these will be explained, analysed and problematised in more detail throughout, it is useful to introduce them as broad concepts:

> **Engagement:** This is the degree to which a learner pays attention to or takes part in an activity. Often, linked to a degree of interest and degrees of motivation, it is also worth noting that learners can engage or not at different levels. For instance, Linnenbrink and Pintrich (2003) distinguish between behaviour, cognitive and motivational engagement. Learners can look like they are engaged in learning, but in reality, they just appear to be without developing their thinking and knowledge in a lesson.

Motivation: This involves working towards a chosen goal in a sustained way (Zimmerman and Schunk, 2008). The principal distinction is between 'intrinsic' and 'extrinsic' motivation. But, as we will see in the work of Ryan and Deci (2000), this is an oversimplification.

Empowerment: Learners have the right to influence their learning, to have ownership of their past, present and future. They have the right to make their voices heard in education. These are enshrined as rights in the United Nations Convention on the Rights of the Child (Detrick, 1999). We see empowerment as more than a political process: as an act of flourishing and the right to achieving one's potential.

Mutuality: This refers to how teaching and learning and teachers and pupils are inextricably linked in the classroom.

Agency: This is the way the learner actively participates in and makes choices that influence their education and the education of others. Everyone has a right to a good education. Everyone has a responsibility to contribute to a good education. Again, this principle stands for teachers as well as pupils.

Who would find this book relevant?

We have written this book with new teachers and early career teachers in mind. We do not believe in the novice–expert dichotomy between new and experienced teachers. Everyone has something to bring to the profession. Sometimes, the youngest and least experienced teachers have creative, innovative and breathtaking learning experiences. Although a teacher may have worked in the same school for 20 years, we value the wisdom but also the desire to learn something new for their own benefit as well as for that of their classes.

For the new teacher, coming to terms with all the activities of the classroom can be a difficult but rewarding time. Often, making sense of this experience follows early periods of training – for instance, in England, by completing a Postgraduate Certificate in Education. Making sense of the pupils' learning is critical. But actually, this can only be achieved by a process of self-examination and self-discovery. Understanding the principals of teacher learning are just as important. We need to learn how to become a teacher in order to learn about a good education.

The process of learning for a new teacher, we believe, is based on the same principles as those for a pupil. Knowledge, skills, understanding, together with social, emotional and ethical development, are at the root of the education of a new teacher. Of course, the language, the activities and the motivations might be different. But becoming a more advanced learner takes commitment to understand explicitly what others might understand only implicitly. Learning really is a journey for both teachers and pupils at so many levels.

Case study examples and how the chapters are organised

At the start of this book, we said that reading is a process of self-discovery. We also see the act of reading as a dialogue between the writer and the reader. Sometimes we talk directly to each other. Sometimes you might agree. Sometimes you might disagree. Sometimes we ask questions to help you learn about education. Sometimes we ask questions to help you learn about yourself. In order to make learning explicit in this book, we have adopted a fairly structured approach in each chapter:

- A chapter guide with a synopsis of the learning focus in the chapter introduction: you will know how the chapter is organised and what you will learn about in the chapter.
- Case studies of fictionalised school examples from both primary and secondary schools. The case studies will help you relate the chapter to your own educational setting and you as a learner. The examples may well be different from or similar to your own experiences, but we want to use them to help you think more deeply about education and your role as a teacher.
- Reflection points explicitly ask you questions about yourself as a teacher and your understanding of key concepts in this book. Reflection can be useful in two ways: understanding what your starting position is before being introduced to new areas; and to reflect on new information after the event. We use both approaches, but of course, you can read this book in different ways. You can come back to the reflection points to perfect your understanding. You might change your perspective as you read this book.

Our aim is to engage, motivate and empower you as a learner.

Making the links to school-based training for teachers

For teachers who are new to the profession and at the stage of gaining their initial qualifications, you will be able to use this book to support your academic and professional studies. In England, the framework that governs the work of teachers is called the Teachers' Standards (Department for

Education (DfE), 2011). They are issued by law. You must follow them unless there is a good reason not to. They define the minimum level of practice for trainees and teachers to achieve qualified teacher status. You can also use them to assess the performance of all teachers with qualified teacher status who are subject to the Education (School Teachers' Appraisal) (England) Regulations 2012.

In England, only graduates can become qualified teachers. In other countries, the requirement is a Master's-level qualification. There are arguments for and against the level of qualification, but there is strong agreement in most governments that teachers should at least have a university degree. Likewise, there is seldom disagreement that much of the early career development to become a teacher should take place in a school. Both schools and universities can contribute to the academic and professional development of the new teacher. As you will see in this book, we do not agree with a false dichotomy that pits schools and universities against each other in the education of new teachers.

To this extent, then, we believe that new teachers, those in their initial training, will benefit both professionally and academically from reading and engaging with this book. It will help you to become a better teacher. It will also help you in your academic essays, professional reflections and development of pedagogical knowledge to become a teacher.

The following overview will help you to understand how the book is organised by chapter, with a summary of the areas covered.

Overview of chapters

Chapter 2 **Staying the course** explains some of the reasons why teachers choose to pursue teaching as a career, and the external and internal factors influencing teachers in the classroom. The role of core reflection in teacher development is explained in the context of the challenges that both trainees and qualified teachers face today. How do teachers achieve a balance in their work and their well-being? What are the practical ways of overcoming some of the key challenges facing educators today?

Chapter 3 **Intrinsic and extrinsic motivation** introduces the traditional distinction between intrinsic and extrinsic motivation. These are related to self-actualisation, autonomy and connectedness for both teachers and pupils. The chapter ends with a discussion of the balance between internal and external reward.

Chapter 4 **Better learning, better behaviour** considers the influence of the relationship between teacher and learner on classroom behaviour. An important factor is the modelling of positive behaviours and the key steps that help to make modelling work in practice. Linked to the last chapter is a discussion of the importance of praise and how the fundamentals of positive psychology can be applied to encourage positive classroom environments. Throughout, there is an explanation of practical ways of dealing with negative behaviours, without compromising the positivity of your classroom ethos. Overall, we reinforce the importance of positivity on a wider level with colleagues and within your broader context.

Chapter 5 **Well-being and safeguarding pupils and teachers** explains the problematic and complex aspects of well-being and safeguarding of pupils and teachers. Risk factors such as accountability without responsibility, isolation, basic needs and cultural needs are all considered, alongside protective factors for well-being and safeguarding in pupils and teachers. The roles of teachers and other professionals in safeguarding is explained.

Chapter 6 **Professional engagement** proposes a framework for engagement, motivation and empowerment that builds a culture of engagement, challenge, interest and self-determination for teachers. Strategies for engaging teachers and developing engaging schools are discussed.

Chapter 7 **Motivating all learners** identifies the learner as an individual and the importance of valuing this individuality. The academic needs of pupils and how to differentiate effectively are balanced with the emotional and pastoral needs of the learner. The potential sociocultural contexts of the learner and how these link to inclusion are suggested as important principles in motivating children and young people.

Chapter 8 **Motivating teachers** explains the current context for initial training and professional development for early career teachers. We should recognise the need for different models of professional development for teachers at different stages of their career. Whilst motivating the teacher is important, we also see the institutional context as being important. What are the characteristics of motivating schools?

Chapter 9 **Active learning** identifies the key concepts at the heart of active learning. These are related to cognitive psychology, with key strategies and how to implement them in your practice. Active learning for pupils and teachers is a critical factor in developing a good education. It is at the centre of engagement, motivation and empowerment.

Chapter 10 **Empowering learners** provides a definition of empowerment as a lifelong learning experience, building learning for life in pupils in empowering school structures. There are suggestions on how to improve and maintain learning through pedagogies of empowerment. Importantly, we suggest that responsibility and accountability are shared between teachers and pupils, for instance by including pupils and teachers in school decision-making.

***Chapter 11* The future: What do we stand for in education?** concludes with a discussion of how our values as early career teachers help build resilience and flourishing in school. The concept of mutuality between pupils and teachers is reinforced as a key principle. Only through this balanced view of the education of both pupils and teachers can we develop a good education.

Chapter summary

- This chapter explains the purpose and readership for this book.
- Key concepts of engagement, motivation, empowerment, agency and mutuality are defined.
- The organisation of each chapter is explained to support early career teachers in engaging with this book: for instance, how case studies and reflection points can be used to develop understanding of schools and you as a teacher.
- Each chapter is summarised to explain key concepts and to preview the content of the book.

Further reading

Bronfenbrenner, U. (1992) *Ecological Systems Theory*. London: Jessica Kingsley Publishers.
A seminal theory of the interaction between the learner and their environment is provided here. It is relevant here because this is exactly the same process for pupils and teachers.

Linnenbrink, E.A. and Pintrich, P.R. (2003) 'The role of self-efficacy beliefs in student engagement and learning in the classroom', *Reading & Writing Quarterly*, 19: 119–37.
This provides an excellent introduction to the concepts of engagement, motivation and self-efficacy as they appear in the classroom.

Bibliography

Bronfenbrenner, U. (1992) *Ecological Systems Theory*. London: Jessica Kingsley Publishers.
Department for Education (DfE) (2011) *Guidance: Teachers' Standards*. London: DfE. Available at: http://www.gov.uk/government/publications/teachers-standards (accessed December 2017).

Detrick, S. (1999) *A Commentary on the United Nations Convention on the Rights of the Child*. Leiden: Martinus Nijhoff Publishers.

Edwards, C.P., Gandini, L. and Forman, G.E. (1998) *The Hundred Languages of Children: The Reggio Emilia Approach – Advanced Reflections*. Westport, CT: Greenwood Publishing Group.

Linnenbrink, E.A. and Pintrich, P.R. (2003) 'The role of self-efficacy beliefs in student engagement and learning in the classroom', *Reading & Writing Quarterly*, 19: 119–37.

Ryan, R.M. and Deci, E.L. (2000) 'Self-determination theory and the facilitation of intrinsic motivation, social development, and well-being', *American Psychologist*, 55 (1): 68–78.

Zimmerman, B.J. and Schunk, D.H. (2008) 'Motivation: An essential dimension of self-regulated learning', in D.H. Schunk and B.J. Zimmerman (eds), *Motivation and Self-Regulated Learning: Theory, Research, and Applications*. Mahwah, NJ: Lawrence Erlbaum Associates Publishers.

2

STAYING THE COURSE

Chapter guide

In this chapter, you will learn about:

- The reasons why teachers choose to pursue teaching as a career
- The external and internal factors influencing teacher efficacy and resilience
- The role of core reflection in teacher development
- The potential role of 'flow' in teacher practice and teacher well-being
- The challenges that both trainees and qualified teachers face today
- Practical ways of overcoming some of the key challenges facing educators today

---

REFLECTION POINT

- What are the most significant challenges you have faced so far as a teacher?
- Where do you see yourself and your teaching career in the future?
- How can you apply some of the strategies in this chapter to your own life so that you can safeguard your own well-being and continue to do a great job as a teacher?

In this chapter, we will explore some of the ways that teachers can 'stay the course' in the face of challenges regardless of their school context or their career stage. Hilton (2017) describes an increasingly bleak (although all too familiar) picture in terms of teacher recruitment and retention in England. She argues that:

> the profession is becoming far less attractive to potential recruits. . . [due to] the lack of status of the profession, the micro-management by government of everything that happens in schools, lack of communication between government departments, coupled with the lack of trust of teachers; constant inspection and a loss of professionalism and the low pay in comparison with other jobs. (Ibid.: 83)

Hilton argues that these factors are causing what is sometimes referred to in the media and in teaching communities as a 'recruitment crisis'. We could explore all of these issues here in more depth; however, this could at least partly undermine our aim to provide a positive and proactive reflection on a variety of educational issues. That is not to say that these factors are not important; in fact, we believe that they represent significant challenges to educators and to society as a whole. However, we are painfully aware of our own limited influence over these factors and recognise that devoting this section of our book to the illustration and exemplification of these challenges to teachers would solve very little.

Instead, we will identify and apply some of the key concepts of positive psychology in order to demonstrate how teachers can 'stay the course' in the face of these challenges. There is no denying how difficult it is to be a teacher, yet we will consider whether in fact this high level of difficulty actually contributes to the high satisfaction rates that many teachers report. We will also explore a process called 'core reflection' in more depth, arguing that if teachers are able to be authentic versions of themselves within the classroom, using their strengths in order to overcome their weaknesses, then they will be happier both personally and professionally. These two spheres are not separate: it is important for teachers to be authentic, self-aware practitioners in order for them to safeguard their own mental and emotional well-being and to enjoy long and rewarding careers.

Why do teachers become teachers?

There are a range of factors that motivate prospective teachers to apply for teacher training programmes and embark upon teaching careers. In the past, motivational factors influencing prospective teachers have been divided into three categories: intrinsic, extrinsic and altruistic.

Intrinsically motivated teachers

Roness explains that 'intrinsically motivated teachers are focused on teaching and the activity related to the job itself. The inherent satisfaction or the joy of teaching is viewed as the driving force' (2011: 629).

Extrinsically motivated teachers

Roness continues by describing how 'extrinsically motivated teachers focus on the benefits of teaching, such as salary, vacations or other external rewards connected to the job' (2011: 629). Pertinently, extrinsic rewards have a high profile in recruitment campaigns within the UK, with the government's 2016 'Get into Teaching' highlighting 'enviable job security and a generous pension' (Department for Education, 2016) as key incentives for choosing a teaching career.

Altruistically motivated teachers

The social dimension of teaching is at work here, with Roness explaining that: 'the altruistically motivated teacher views teaching as a socially worthwhile and important job, and has a desire to be part of young peoples' growth and development' (2011: 629).

While the aforementioned three categories provide us with a useful starting point for considering the reasons why people decide to embark upon a teaching career, they have been criticised as consisting of specific and individual motivational factors that interlink and overlap, leading to a lack of precision if prospective teachers are assigned a category that may not reflect the intricacies of their own reasons for entering teaching. Richardson and Watt criticise earlier studies of teacher motivation, arguing that 'prior research has lacked an integrative theoretical framework to guide the selection and organization of influential factors, proceeded in a somewhat piecemeal fashion using poorly defined constructs, and with individual researchers frequently investigating subsets of possible factors' (2006: 31). This evaluation led to the development of the Factors Influencing Teaching Choice scale (FIT-Choice), which aimed 'to provide a comprehensive and coherent model to guide systematic investigation into the question of why people choose a teaching career' (ibid.). Their model is rooted in the expectancy theory of motivation, 'which argues that individuals' choices and behaviours are shaped by their expectancies and their values' (Watt and Richardson, 2008: 410).

Interestingly, many of the most popular reasons for embarking upon a teaching career are common across a number of different countries. Watt et al. (2012) used the FIT-Choice scale to analyse a range of international samples from Australia, the USA, Germany and Norway. In their study, they found that 'the highest rated motivations for the choice of a teaching career were consistently intrinsic value, perceived teaching ability, the desire to make a social contribution, to work with children/adolescents, and having had positive prior teaching and learning experiences' (ibid.: 804).

Intrinsic value of teaching

The intrinsic value of teaching can be seen as relating to the pleasure or enjoyment that a teacher gains from their role. These intrinsic factors can be seen as rooted in the prospective teacher's conception of themselves and their key qualities as well as their own personal understanding of the remit of a teacher's role.

Perceived teaching ability

A prospective trainee's perception of their own abilities as a teacher can push them towards the profession. This obviously is again tied to the prospective teacher's own preconceptions as to what the role entails, and can therefore be linked to their own prior teaching and learning experiences. This also links to Csikszentmihalyi's 'flow' theory (2002), which sees the perfect balance between the perceived level of challenge and the perceived ability as leading to a 'flow' state that is associated with high levels of well-being and creativity. The idea of 'flow' links the perceived teaching ability to the intrinsic value of teaching in that it could be argued that it is the balance between ability and challenge that creates pleasure or enjoyment.

The desire to make a social contribution

Watt et al. (2012) report an interesting finding in terms of motivations of pre-service teachers in Norway. They argue that:

> because of Norway's egalitarian principles of unity and equality in school . . . we had anticipated that there would be less perceived need for interventions to target structural social and educational inequities, and consequently that the Norwegian participants would be less

motivated to pursue teaching for reasons related to social utility. In support of this hypothesis, the Norwegian sample did indeed score significantly lowest on all of the social utility factors. (Ibid.: 803)

In this way, it could be argued that the desire to make a social contribution is a key driving force for prospective teachers in countries where social and educational inequalities are more prevalent.

The desire to work with children or adolescents

Many teachers across the globe rate the desire to work with children or adolescents as highly influential in their decision to pursue careers in teaching. Richardson and Watt see this motivational factor as part of the '"social utility value" construct' (2006: 32), linking this with other motivations such as the desire to 'shape [the] future of children/adolescents', 'enhance social equity' and 'make [a] social contribution' (ibid.).

Positive prior teaching and learning experiences

Watt et al. found that:

> prior experiences of positive teaching and learning rated quite high (particularly in the US), which may be particular to the choice of teaching as a career. Because almost every individual has been a student, effective (and ineffective) teachers can provide powerful role models, as well as the opportunity for vicarious personal judgements concerning one's own teaching-related abilities. (2012: 804)

What motivates prospective teachers across the globe?

Watt et al.'s view that 'the desire for job security, to enhance social equity, and for choosing teaching because of its provision for family time were rated consistently lower' (2012: 804) highlights that, in many countries, these extrinsic motivations for entering teaching are less important to prospective teachers. However, Thomson et al. (2012) highlight that sociocultural differences are a crucial aspect of motivation by summarising a number of studies that found that extrinsic motivations were more important: 'Studies conducted in Brunei (Yong, 1995), Zimbabwe

(Chivore, 1998), Cameroon (Abangma, 1981), and Jamaica (Bastick, 1999) have found that more extrinsic motivations such as salary, job security, and career status are important for choosing the teaching career' (ibid.: 326), and they highlighted a contrast with studies 'conducted with preservice and inservice teachers in France, Australia, Belgium, Canada, the Netherlands, Slovakia, Estonia, Cyprus and the UK' (ibid.: 325), where an emphasis on 'altruistic reasons and enjoyment in working with children . . . [as well as] individual intellectual fulfilment and making a social contribution were also listed high among reasons to teach' (ibid.).

Perceived ability, perceived challenge and flow

In this section, we will explore the potential of Mihaly Csikszentmihalyi's theory of 'flow'. In their study of flow in the context of the learning environment for high-ability learners, Scager et al. defined flow as: 'a state of intrinsic motivation in which people are fully engaged in a task for the sake of the activity itself' (2014: 660). The idea of the flow state is immediately recognisable for many people who find themselves so immersed in a task that they lose track of time. The application of the concept within the classroom has several potential benefits. First, by motivating learners and teachers intrinsically, a culture of self-development and aspiration can be cultivated. Whilst there has been considerable debate over the idea that extrinsic rewards can undermine intrinsic motivation, Deci et al. conducted a meta-analysis of 128 experiments and concluded that: 'expected tangible rewards did significantly and substantially undermine intrinsic motivation, and this effect was quite robust' (2001: 3). A move from externally regulated extrinsic motivation to self-regulated intrinsic motivation is also linked to higher-quality conceptual learning (Benware and Deci, 1984; Vansteenkiste et al., 2006).

Similarly, the idea of the flow state is inherently individualised and personalised, reflecting the goal of personalisation for many education systems, from New Labour's focus on personalisation as part of their increased marketisation of education in the early 2000s in the UK to the wider acceptance of this in other Western societies as a way to mirror a growing trend in public services towards 'mass customization' (Hargreaves, 2005, quoted in Prain et al., 2013: 656). Whilst there is some debate over the legitimacy of these political roots of personalisation as an educational goal (Harris and Ranson, 2005), there is also significant support for this educational approach and it has arguably been widely embraced by policy-makers and educators in the West (Prain et al., 2013). The internally regulated nature of intrinsic motivation, coupled with the implications of the flow state for well-being, give us a more humanistic foundation for developing a model of personalisation that is rooted in a conception of learning as individual and intrinsically enjoyable, as opposed to attempting to reflect market forces in educational approaches.

High challenge and flow theory

As a teacher, you will know that there are few moments that can compare to the feeling of satisfaction when a learner has a 'light-bulb moment' and suddenly grasps a concept, idea or skill that has previously troubled them. There is a sense of validation for both teacher and learner – the shared journey has been successful and both parties can revel in the result. Korthagen (2013) conceptualises the flow state within the classroom and builds on Csikszentmihalyi's theory in order to provide these moments with a broader definition. He describes these moments as being examples of 'a phenomenon called "shining eyes"', which occurs 'when students are enjoying new challenges, but feel they can deal with them' (ibid.: 25). Perhaps it is the strength of this feeling, alongside its frequency in effective classrooms, which could partly account for high rates of teacher satisfaction despite concerns surrounding workload and conditions. Korthagen argues that:

> when people are in flow, they learn easily and rapidly. It is as if learning becomes something natural, just like in the joyful learning that we can sometimes observe in young children. When there is flow in the process, concentration on the here-and-now, enthusiasm, openness, motivation, and cognitive understanding all go together. (Ibid.)

Similarly, Basom and Frase, in an early exploration of the potential applications of flow theory in the classroom, identified that 'teachers perceived either that their flow caused students to be engaged or that the engagement of students in what the teacher was doing caused the teacher's flow experience' (2004: 244). The interconnected nature of the flow state is interesting here and provides further evidence that the well-being of learners and students is interconnected. Therefore, we could suggest tentatively that an emphasis on the flow state for learners and teachers could be a valuable way to 'stay the course' despite the challenges that teachers face.

Watt and Richardson found that 'individuals who viewed teaching as a highly expert career on entry to teacher education planned to exert greater effort . . . undertake more professional development, persist longer, and aspire to leadership positions in schools' (2007: 167). In an international study, Watt et al. also found that 'perceptions of teaching as an expert career and a high demand career exhibited positive, albeit weak, relationships with satisfaction' (2012: 800). It is therefore possible to tentatively link these findings to the concept of flow, suggesting that this could be an important underlying aspect of the teaching experience that continues to engage, motivate and empower teachers. In this way, the high level of demand that prospective teachers associate with teaching, coupled with their own per-ceived level of ability to deal with this, could be linked to their future potential to experience flow states within their teaching careers and thereby contribute to their own levels of motivation.

REFLECTION POINT

- What motivated you to pursue a career in education?
- Do your motivations fit neatly into one of the three categories outlined at the start of this chapter: intrinsic, extrinsic, altruistic?
- Are these motivations common amongst your colleagues? Whilst it might be difficult to accurately ascertain your colleagues' reasons for pursuing teaching as a career, it may be a worthwhile topic of staffroom conversation.
- Have you ever experienced a 'flow state'? For instance, when you are so absorbed in a task that you lose track of time?
- Have you ever experienced a lesson in which you could retrospectively identify the 'flow state' or 'shining eyes' phenomenon in your learners?

Core reflection for effective teaching and learning

The worthiness of teachers' motivations for entering the profession should be celebrated, particularly as 'the motivations that related most strongly to high initial career satisfaction included the altruistic-type motivations' (Watt et al., 2012: 792). The reasons behind the decisions of trainees to enter the teaching profession are clearly important as they can impact upon both teacher satisfaction and retention. As teachers, it is often interesting to take a step back from our daily roles and to consider which of our qualities help us to be effective practitioners. Coe et al. outline six 'common compo-nents suggested by research that teachers should consider when assessing teaching quality' (2014: 2–3). These are:

- Pedagogical content knowledge
- Quality of instruction
- Classroom climate
- Classroom management
- Teacher beliefs
- Professional behaviours.

Whilst these provide a useful framework for considering our own skills as teachers, it is important to delve deeper into these components and consider how they link to our core values as individuals. Korthagen emphasises the importance of the self in education through an approach to teacher development called 'core reflection', which 'focuses on people's strengths as the springboard for personal growth' (2013: xi). In Chapter 4, we will explore the potential of this emphasis on core qualities in developing positive relationships with learners. Here, however, we will highlight some of the benefits of identifying and celebrating our own core qualities as individuals within our teaching, improving our self-efficacy and our confidence as practitioners. We will explore how knowing our own strengths can help us to 'stay the course'.

Core qualities and teacher development

In highlighting some general characteristics of teachers at the start of this chapter, there is a danger that we could present teachers as a homogeneous group, lacking in individuality. Far from it, we believe that it is important to value teachers as individuals, celebrating their diverse traits and idiosyncrasies alongside the diverse ways in which these can benefit their roles as teachers. In order to explore these individual core qualities, we will refer to those outlined by the Values in Action Institute on Character, based on the work of Peterson and Seligman (2004). The Values in Action (VIA) classification of strengths is shown in Table 2.1.

Table 2.1 The Values in Action classification (based on Peterson and Seligman, 2004)

Creativity	Curiosity	Judgement	Love of learning
Perspective	Bravery	Perseverance	Honesty
Zest	Love	Kindness	Social intelligence
Teamwork	Fairness	Leadership	Forgiveness
Humility	Prudence	Self-regulation	Appreciation of beauty and excellence
Gratitude	Hope	Humour	Spirituality

Whilst there are other classifications of character strengths and qualities, for instance the Organisation for Economic Co-operation and Development's (OECD) 2005 'Definition and Selection of Key Competencies' (DeSeCo) framework, the VIA classification still provides a very useful model for guiding core reflection, allowing us to concentrate on our strength of character rather than our perceived weaknesses. This approach embraces 'positive psychology' (Seligman and Csikszentmihalyi, 2000), rather than reinforcing a deficiency-focused model. In terms of the potential for utilising these core qualities within our own understanding of ourselves as teachers, the diversity of the varying strengths highlights a key strength in itself: we are all very different and these differences should be celebrated and harnessed. Some teachers will rely on their love of learning to inspire their pupils, modelling an intellectual curiosity unsurpassed by their peers; others may demonstrate an awe-inspiring commitment to achieving excellence in all that they and their pupils do, driven by the core quality of appreciation of beauty and excellence. With a framework like the VIA classification, we have the opportunity as teachers both to identify and to value our diversity (see Figure 2.1).

CASE STUDY

In a secondary school in the north of England, a middle leader, in this case a Head of Faculty, used core reflection as part of mentoring an early career stage teacher (newly qualified teacher, or NQT). The early career stage teacher was experiencing some significant problems with the classroom behaviour of her students and was reaching a stage of exasperation that she had not come across before in her experience of teaching. Her determined attitude towards improving the standard of behaviour had led her to read widely and consult a number of colleagues in order to explore possible strategies. Frustratingly, she found that each strategy she tried met with failure and she began to question her own suitability for teaching. Through conducting the VIA survey, which revealed the NQT's core quality of perseverance, her mentor was able to use weekly mentor meetings as an opportunity to reframe her thwarted efforts as examples of her tireless efforts to improve, which simultaneously gave the NQT belief in her own ability to stay the course despite the problems that she was facing: she knew that she could persevere in the long term because this was part of her personality. In turn, her haphazard approach to behaviour for learning became more consistent as her confidence in herself grew, and her feelings of frustration became tempered by her own sense of endurance and strength at having persevered for so long in the face of challenge.

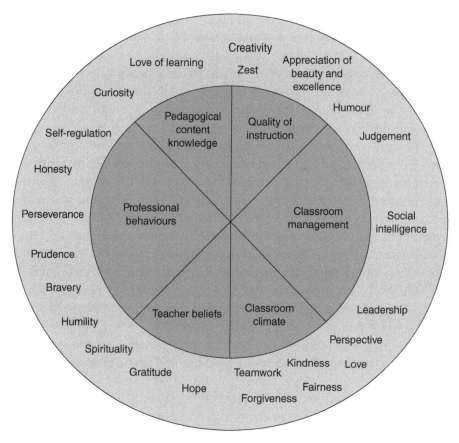

Figure 2.1   The VIA character strengths are mapped onto Coe et al.'s (2014) components of good teaching

So, how do these core values manifest in our approach to teaching? Educator and author Stephen Covey foregrounded the importance of personal values within leadership (personal and work-based), encouraging his readers and students to 'begin with the end in mind . . . with my values and directions clear'. Covey argued that by basing decisions and choices on your values, 'you are proactively choosing what you determine to be the best alternative . . . [and] what you choose to do contributes to your ultimate values in life' (2004: 135). We can apply this idea or principle of character-driven decision-making to the decisions that teachers make on a daily basis. If teachers have a clearly defined and articulated idea of themselves and their own mission statement, then they can use this to drive their own sense of self as an educator.

A key protective factor in maintaining a satisfying teaching career could be your own beliefs about your agency and proactiveness as an individual.

The idea of the agency of the individual is a key aspect of both core reflection and Covey's approach to personal leadership. Covey draws a distinction between the 'circle of influence', which features all the aspects of our lives over which we have some control, and the 'circle of concern', which features those elements that can affect us but over which we have little control. Covey further clarifies the importance of these to personal leadership by distinguishing between 'proactive people [who] focus their efforts in the circle of influence [and] reactive people [who] focus their efforts in the circle of concern' (ibid.: 90). Interestingly, these circles of influence and concern could provide the opportunity for teachers to re-evaluate their own degree of proactiveness. It is true that teachers are often governed by external curricular or government-based guidance (such as national curriculum or exam board qualification specifications), so this aspect of teaching could be categorised within the 'circle of concern'. However, the way that teachers deliver this content could be categorised within the teacher's 'circle of influence'. It is when this autonomy over teacher methodology is compromised that teachers can become disenfranchised and disempowered, a significant challenge to overcome at any stage of your career.

Within many systems of teacher training across the world, trainee teachers are taught pedagogical knowledge and then observed in their teaching, often being judged against national or institutional criteria. It could be argued that in emphasising the importance of this set criteria, trainee teachers are implicitly encouraged to believe in an external locus of control, for example the power that their university or school-based tutor has over their ability to pass a teacher training programme. Rather than solely focusing on a wider set of teaching standards, trainees could also be supported to work outwards from their own core qualities in order to hypothesise as to the kinds of teacher qualities they could manifest. For instance, as a trainee teacher, you could identify your own core strengths and then apply these to the classroom, identifying ways in which these could be useful. This process could then be used to aid your own self-reflection (Table 2.2). Have you demonstrated the outcomes that you thought you would? Have you fulfilled the potential of your core strength within the classroom?

Challenges facing teachers

In the spirit of a positive, proficiency-focused approach to 'staying the course', we will explore challenges by first operationalising strengths. As already mentioned, the OECD's DeSeCo (1993) outlines three categories for key competencies:

Table 2.2 An illustration of some of the practical classroom applications of the core strength, 'Appreciation of beauty and excellence'

Core strength	Classroom application What does this look like in practice?
Appreciation of beauty and excellence	• High expectations of learners • High-quality resources are produced (well presented, high levels of accuracy, Standard English, etc.) • Enthusiasm for achievements within your subject specialism (e.g., a reverence for Isaac Newton that is communicated passionately to learners within a science lesson on gravity) • A strong sense of what the highest-quality outcome would look like for learners • Efforts to enable all learners to reach the highest-quality outcome possible within the lesson

- Using tools interactively
- Interacting in heterogeneous groups
- Acting autonomously.

In a study in 2012, Iluz et al. adapted the key competencies within the DeSeCo framework in order to devise a '35-Item Life Challenges Teacher Inventory, which was derived from the three theoretical competencies identified by the DeSeCo model' (ibid.: 51). The inventory includes some of the competencies listed in Table 2.3.

Working from these competencies, challenges to teachers can be seen as any deficiency, incident, policy or event that compromises any of the

Table 2.3 Key competencies

Using tools interactively	Interacting in heterogenous groups	Acting autonomously
1. I can present a new concept that I am learning in a variety of ways.	13. Team cooperation gives me a sense of security at work.	22. When I learn, I reconsider what I've already read or heard about the topic in order to decide if the new learning material convinces me.
5. I have a sense of mastery over the contents I teach.	17. When I am faced with different alternatives, I have no difficulty in making a decision.	26. I know how to focus and consolidate the goals of educational initiatives.
6. I have a sense of mastery over the skills in the discipline I teach.	21. When I set myself a goal, I meet it.	30. I can estimate the future results of initiatives.

Note: For the full inventory, see Iluz et al. (2012).

above competencies. For instance, competency 32 refers to appreciation from the administration – be this the faculty, school, local authority or national educational organisation within which a teacher works. If the teacher does not receive this appreciation, then it could be seen as a challenge. Similarly, with competency 30 focusing on the ability to foresee the effects of key actions, a challenge to teachers could be a system in which endlessly changing expectations of their work destabilise their ability to make realistic predictions. These challenges can be individually experienced, perhaps by one teacher working in a school, or more universally impactful, perhaps affecting a large number of teachers within a particular organisation or even country. For instance, in an overview of the challenges and opportunities that the education sector in Tanzania faces, Lee highlights the 'strong positive relationship . . . between resource allocation and educational outcomes' (2015: 113). This suggests, initially, that a lack of resources is a significant challenge for a number of teachers in the country (ibid.). However, what Lee also highlights is that the impact of a lack of resources is not the only challenge facing teachers and that this is not the only factor contributing to patterns of attainment. Lee explains that 'unequal spending and social conditions cannot explain all the variation in educational outcomes. The empirical evidence suggests substantial inefficiencies in some districts, which are most likely related to local managerial effectiveness and/or teachers' incentives' (ibid.:113). Within this context, the multifarious nature of educational challenges is foregrounded, and, as educational professionals, the gauntlet is thrown down for us to devise ways to safeguard teacher well-being and educational effectiveness in the face of sometimes numerous, fluctuating challenges.

In many countries across the world, teaching is heavily politicised and therefore affected by political changes within particular societies. It could be argued, however, that these changes can be less likely to cause harm if they still honour the competencies that are central to teachers' professional growth. For argument's sake, whilst a lack of funding for schools is often highlighted as a key issue, it could be claimed that as long as funding is sufficient for teachers to fulfil the competencies above, then this is less likely to have a negative impact on teachers. By contrast, and perhaps more logically, there is an implicit reliance on a relatively high standard of funding in a range of the competencies explored in the inventory, for instance in the emphasis on 'advanced technologies', 'libraries', 'databases', 'seminars, educational field trips, exhibits' and so on. For an early career stage teacher anywhere in the world, the competencies provide us with a degree of insight into what professional well-being looks like for teachers.

Tackling challenges

So, if the challenges faced by teachers can be individual and highly changeable, then it is important to develop a range of strategies in order to deal with these effectively.

Teachers taking personal responsibility

Whenever you teach your class or classes, you are exercising your own agency and professional judgement as an educational practitioner. It might not always feel like it, but it is important to remember that your classroom is your domain. Early on in your career, you might feel a little tentative in asserting your particular core values. However, it is still important to reflect philosophically on your own key strengths as a teacher, for instance in terms of the VIA survey or Iluz et al.'s (2012) competencies framework, and to then think about your own beliefs as an educator.

We raise a note of caution here. We are not referring to arguably superficial beliefs, for instance a conviction in the importance of attractive resources, but rather, we are seeking the identification of the value judgements at work in your classroom behind the scenes. There is danger in de facto rules and generalisations. For instance, the teacher who asserts that 'group work is always superior to individual work as it helps students to develop interpersonal skills' is potentially reducing their own values to unhelpful, regressive soundbites that actually do a disservice to their wider aims and beliefs. If this teacher believes that interpersonal skills are important, then this could well be a core value at the heart of their practice as an educator. However, by asserting the supremacy of group work over individual work at all times in all circumstances without exception, the teacher limits their own classroom tools in devising tasks that are effective. In education, as with other disciplines relating to human beings, it is difficult to establish universal truths or principles as people are so different. The classroom environment is such a complex, multifaceted setting that to make sweeping assertions about tools that are effective and tools that are not, with little evidence, can be damaging to our own confidence in being effective practitioners. In a study by Retnowati et al., the authors commented that 'though no superior effect was found for group work compared with individual study, no significant negative effects were found either' (2010: 363), suggesting that both of these methods have their places within our classrooms.

Such pragmatism flies in the face of many educators who seek to reignite the battle between 'traditional' and 'progressive' approaches to education. Gerard Guthrie, in his controversial work *The Progressive Education Fallacy in*

Developing Countries, outlines his perception of the differences between a traditional (or formalistic) approach versus a progressive approach to education:

> Formalistic classrooms are constructed around the teachers' pedagogical role as an expert who transmits or reveals culturally valued knowledge as a product. Progressive classrooms centre around students' culturally-defined learning processes, in particular the view that students should discover or construct their own knowledge from a young age, which the teacher facilitates. (2011: 4)

This debate was summarised through the medium of rhyme in Alison King's terms 'sage on the stage' and 'guide on the side' in 1993. The first term reflects the formalistic or traditional approach, whilst the second supposedly reflects the progressive approach. Whilst there are various views relating to this debate, it seems counterproductive to jump on a bandwagon and make assertions at the expense of choice. Perhaps this view of the importance of choice is rooted in Western liberal values that emphasise the importance of individualism, but if freedom and choice are values that you feel are important, then maybe you too will feel somewhat disconcerted by any educational debate that seeks to limit the pedagogical methods at the teacher's disposal.

Flow and protective factors

There are many challenges that teachers face at all stages of their careers. However, as we discussed earlier, the high level of challenge at the heart of the teacher's work can, in fact, offer potential rewards such as the promotion of the 'flow' state. Habe and Tement argued that 'workload by itself does not diminish work flow. In fact, support was found for a motivation-promotion role of workload' (2016: 35). In this way, it is not the amount of work that teachers have to do that poses a problem, but the way in which this work is perhaps organised, approached or managed that could potentially become a challenge.

Connectedness, autonomy and self-actualisation

In Chapter 5, we will discuss how the quality of relationships (connectedness), personal and professional control (autonomy) and ultimately personal growth (self-actualisation) are significant aspects of well-being for pupils and teachers. For the time being, we will briefly outline some of the ways in which these three factors can enable teachers to 'stay the course'.

Connectedness

Tse et al. (2016) explored how teamwork and flow proneness can actually help individuals to combat the effects of excessive challenges in their workplace. The study found that the 'negative association [between excessive challenge and flow state] can be mitigated if people work as a team' (ibid.: 287). Similarly, Tse et al. found that: 'playing as a team with high interdependence among team members provided better enjoyment and experience' (ibid.: 287). As an early career stage teacher, you may not yet be formally responsible for leading a team within your educational setting. However, we can all take responsibility for the roles that we play in teams regardless of our career stage. Similarly, 'bottom-up' approaches to teacher development can be hugely effective in improving teaching and learning.

CASE STUDY

In a Leicestershire high school, an NQT introduced a teacher sharing session, having proposed this to the Senior Leadership Team as a way of sharing good practice and encouraging wider reflection on teaching and learning approaches across different subject areas. The 'bottom-up' nature of the strategy, alongside the low-stakes format of sharing teaching ideas over a cup of coffee in the staffroom, meant that teachers did not perceive this as an additional burden, but instead were impressed and energised by the enthusiasm of the NQT who took the lead on the 'Fifteen Minute Forum'. There are examples of such approaches in many schools, with varying degrees of effectiveness. In exploring such approaches, we recommend that examples of good practice are always grounded in the ways that they contribute to high-quality learning, with a thoughtful and deep analysis of how this is exemplified in practice. A superficial sharing of 'top tips' or attractive resources that are produced for solely aesthetic rather than educational purposes is unlikely to be effective.

The 2013 Teaching and Learning International Survey (TALIS) reported that:

teachers who collaborate more with their colleagues – teaching jointly in the same class, observing and providing feedback on each other's classes, engaging in joint activities across different classes and age groups, and taking part in collaborative professional learning – report a greater sense of self-efficacy. (OECD, 2014: 23)

The advent of new technologies such as social media also present teachers with the opportunity to collaborate with others beyond their own school and geographical areas. The social media platform Twitter is used by a vast number of teachers in order to share a whole host of educational resources through the use of hashtags (the index system which allows users to view posts that are linked to a particular topic). For example, a number of users established the hashtag #teamenglish in order to publicly share resources that had been produced by individual teachers or English faculties. Obviously, there are clear implications for teacher workload here, with teachers being able to access the resources of others rather than creating their own 'from scratch'. Similarly, there is an opportunity to discuss and reflect on particular resources, approaches or strategies with a wider range of practitioners than may be available in the typical staffroom. Davis conducted a study of teachers' perceptions of Twitter as a tool for professional development in the USA (focusing on the hashtag #EdChat), and argued that 'through archived documents and participant interviews, results of the study indicated that teachers used the online forum as a way to share knowledge and resources, and as a place to experience emotional support from colleagues' (2015: 1557). However, social media sharing is not without its problems.

Autonomy

Autonomy, defined by Habe and Tement (2016) as 'employees' freedom in scheduling their work and in determining work methods', is a crucial aspect of well-being and can be seen as an important protective factor for teachers at any stage of their career. Skaalvik and Skaalvik give us greater insight into the role of autonomy within the teaching profession with their explanation that: 'teacher autonomy may concern the freedom to choose goals, teaching methods, and educational strategies that are concordant with the teacher's personal educational beliefs and values' (2014: 69).

Habe and Tement argued that 'autonomy and variety were found to enhance absorption, work enjoyment and intrinsic work motivation' (2016: 30), demonstrating the positive impact that autonomy can have. For teachers, this poses questions relating to the key aims of many schools in terms of providing consistency for learners. In the pursuit of consistency, some schools adopt a conformity-focused approach, which could potentially undermine the autonomy of individual classroom teachers if they are not given the freedom outlined by Skaalvik and Skaalvik above. Therefore, it is important for a teacher to work in a school that harmonises with their 'personal educational beliefs and values' (Skaalvik and Skaalvil, 2014: 69) so that the teacher does not find themselves in a position where their beliefs and values are being ignored by the school institution, resulting in their autonomy being challenged.

However, Skaalvik and Skaalvik explore an interesting aspect of the relationship between teacher autonomy and engagement by comparing teachers who identified as having a high level of self-efficacy and teachers who identified as having a low level of self-efficacy. In this way, the impact of high levels of autonomy on a confident teacher as opposed to an unconfident teacher are highlighted. Skaalvik and Skaalvik argued that: 'teachers with strong mastery expectations may perceive autonomy as an opportunity to teach according to their own values, to use their resources, to experiment with new practices, and to change practices according to the situation and to the students' needs' (2014: 76). In contrast:

> for teachers with low mastery expectations, autonomy may provide an opportunity to avoid challenges and to hide self-perceived deficits and shortcomings. This is a self-protective strategy that may increase engagement and job satisfaction and decrease emotional exhaustion in the short run. But avoiding challenges may also represent a barrier to personal learning and development. In the long run, autonomy may therefore not be beneficial for learning and development for teachers with low mastery expectations. (Ibid.)

We feel that a high level of autonomy, accompanied by a strong sense of interconnectedness – which means that teachers can draw on support and advice from other practitioners in an honest and open way – is the most practical solution to this double-edged sword. In a high-stakes accountability system, some schools may be too frightened of the impact of providing autonomy for teachers with lower mastery expectations. It is up to us to develop supportive systems that enable all teachers to thrive and teach authentically.

Personal growth and self-actualisation

By embracing the core reflection model, teachers can directly and indirectly tie their personal growth to their professional development. There is a lot to be said for self-understanding and self-actualisation, and the process of reflecting on your own core qualities and the role that they play in your life and work can be transformative.

The overarching message here is that teachers are human beings and should be valued as such within the educational systems in which they work. Teaching can be a truly life-affirming career, but, in order for pro-spective and early career stage teachers to 'stay the course', they need to be engaged, motivated and empowered.

Chapter summary

- There are many challenges facing teachers that can affect recruitment and retention rates.
- The motivations for choosing teaching as a career can be very different for different individuals. Roness (2011) argues that teachers can be:
  - intrinsically motivated and therefore focused on the inherent satis-faction that they experience when teaching
  - extrinsically motivated and concerned with external rewards such as salary
  - altruistically motivated and therefore committed to the social wor-thiness of their role and their perception of its importance to the lives of young people and wider society.
- Richardson and Watt (2006) devised a Factors Influencing Teaching Choice scale so as to sharpen these definitions of the reasons why teachers go into teaching. These reasons include:
  - intrinsic value of teaching
  - perceived teaching ability
  - the desire to make a social contribution
  - the desire to work with children and adolescents
  - positive prior teaching and learning experiences.
- The perception that teaching is a challenging career means that it is likely to meet many of the conditions for Csikszentmihalyi's flow state (2002), which is a state of intrinsic motivation, in which the individual loses track of time and gains enjoyment from simply carrying out a particular task. The flow state is associated with well-being, and therefore increased instances of flow whilst teaching have the potential to safeguard teacher well-being and help teachers to 'stay the course'.
- Teachers may find it worthwhile to identify their own core qualities (Korthagen, 2013; Peterson and Seligman, 2004) and to explicitly draw on these strengths in their approach to teaching. This has the potential to be a powerful, proficiency-focused tool for reflection and continued improvement.
- Iluz et al. (2012) devised an inventory of life challenges that may be faced by teachers. These can give us an indication of what pressures teachers might face and why these pressures can affect teacher well-being.

- Teachers can safeguard their well-being by:
  - embracing the autonomy that they do have within their classroom
  - forming supportive connections with colleagues
  - using positive psychology approaches such as core reflection in order to place an emphasis on personal growth and self-actualisation.

Further reading

Csikszentmihalyi, M. (2002) *Flow: The Classic Work on How to Achieve Happiness*. London: Rider.
This provides a deeper exploration of the implications of Csikszentmihalyi's flow state for well-being.

Korthagen, F.A.J., Kim, Y.M. and Greene, W.L. (eds) (2013) *Teaching and Learning from Within: A Core Reflection Approach to Quality and Inspiration in Education*. New York: Routledge.
If you are interested in learning more about core strengths and how these can be used in your teaching, then you may be interested in this.

Bibliography

Basom, M.R. and Frase, L. (2004) 'Creating optimal work environments: Exploring teacher flow experiences', *Mentoring & Tutoring: Partnership in Learning*, 12 (2): 241–58.

Benware, C.A. and Deci, E.L. (1984) 'Quality of learning with an active versus passive motivational set', *American Educational Research Journal*, 21 (4): 755–65.

Coe, R., Aloisi, C., Higgins, S. and Major, L.E. (2014) *What Makes Great Teaching? Review of the Underpinning Research*. Durham and London: Centre for Evaluation and Monitoring (CEM), Durham University, and The Sutton Trust. Available at: http://www.suttontrust.com/wp-content/uploads/2014/10/What-Makes-Great-Teaching-REPORT.pdf (accessed 31 December 2017).

Covey, S.R. (2004) *The 7 Habits of Highly Effective People: Powerful Lessons in Personal Change*. New York: Free Press.

Csikszentmihalyi, M. (2002) *Flow: The Classic Work on How to Achieve Happiness*. London: Rider.

Davis, K. (2015) 'Teachers' perceptions of Twitter for professional development', *Disability and Rehabilitation*, 37 (17): 1551–8.

Deci, E.L., Koestner, R. and Ryan, R.M. (2001) 'Extrinsic rewards and intrinsic motivation in education: Reconsidered once again', *Review of Educational Research*, 71 (1): 1–27.

Department for Education (2016) 'Get into Teaching: Support and Advice from the Department for Education'. Available at: https://getintoteaching.education.gov.uk/why-teach (accessed 9 April 2016).

Guthrie, G. (2011) *The Progressive Education Fallacy in Developing Countries.* New York: Springer.

Habe, K. and Tement, S. (2016) 'Flow among higher education teachers: A job demands-resources perspective', *Psihološka Obzorja/Horizons in Psychology,* 25: 29–37.

Harris, A. and Ranson, S. (2005) 'The contradictions of education policy: Disadvantage and achievement', *British Educational Research Journal,* 31 (5): 571–87.

Hilton, G. (2017) 'Disappearing teachers: An exploration of a variety of views as to the causes of the problems affecting teacher recruitment and retention in England', in N. Popov et al. (eds),) *Current Business and Economics Driven Discourse and Education: Perspectives from Around the World: BCES Conference Books Volume 15,* Sofia: Bulgarian Comparative Education Society.

Iluz, S., Michalsky, T. and Kramarski, B. (2012) 'Developing and assessing the Life Challenges Teacher Inventory for teachers' professional growth', *Studies in Educational Evaluation,* 38 (2): 44–54.

Kerry, D. (2015) 'Teachers' perceptions of Twitter for professional development', *Disability and Rehabilitation,* 37 (17): 1551–8.

King, A. (1993) 'From Sage on the Stage to Guide on the Side', *College Teaching,* 41 (1): 30–5.

Korthagen, F.A.J. (2013) 'The core reflection approach', in F.A.J. Korthagen, Y.M. Kim and W.L. Greene (eds), *Teaching and Learning from Within: A Core Reflection Approach to Quality and Inspiration in Education.* New York: Routledge.

Lee, S. (2015) 'Value for money in education', in A.R. Joshi and I. Gaddis (eds), *Preparing the Next Generation in Tanzania: Challenges and Opportunities in Education.* Washington, DC: World Bank Publications.

OECD (2005) *'Definition and Selection of Key Competencies: Executive Summary'.* Available at: http://deseco.ch/bfs/deseco/en/index/02.html (accessed 28 September 2018)

Organisation for Economic Co-operation and Development (OECD) (2014) A Teachers' Guide to TALIS 2013: Teaching and Learning International Survey. Paris: OECD. Available at: http:// www.oecd.org/education/a-teachers-guide-to-talis-2013-9789264216075-en.htm (accessed 31 December 2017).

Peterson, C. and Seligman, M. (2004) *Character Strengths and Virtues: A Handbook and Classification.* New York: Oxford University Press and Washington, DC: American Psychological Association.

Prain, V. et al. (2013) 'Personalised learning: Lessons to be learnt', *British Educational Research Journal,* 39 (4): 654–76.

Retnowati, E., Ayres, P. and Sweller, J. (2010) 'Worked example effects in individual and group work settings', *An International Journal of Experimental Educational Psychology,* 30 (3): 349–67.

Richardson, P.W. and Watt, H.M.G. (2006) 'Who chooses teaching and why? Profiling characteristics and motivations across three Australian universities', *Asia-Pacific Journal of Teacher Education,* 34 (1): 27–56.

Roness, D. (2011) 'Still motivated? The motivation for teaching during the second year in the profession', *Teaching and Teacher Education,* 27 (3): 628–38.

Scager, K., Akkerman, S.S., Pilot, A. and Wubbels, T. (2014) 'Challenging high-ability learners', *Studies in Higher Education*, 39 (4): 659–79.

Seligman, M.E. and Csikszentmihalyi, M. (2000) 'Positive psychology: An introduction', *The American Psychologist*, 55 (1): 5–14.

Skaalvik, E.M. and Skaalvik, S. (2014) 'Teacher self-efficacy and perceived autonomy: Relations with teacher engagement, job satisfaction, and emotional exhaustion', *Psychological Reports*, 114: 68–77.

Thomson, M.M., Turner, J.E. and Nietfeld, J.L. (2012) 'A typological approach to investigate the teaching career decision: Motivations and beliefs about teaching of prospective teacher candidates', *Teaching and Teacher Education*, 28 (3): 324–35.

Tse, D. C. K., Fung, H., Nakamura, J. and Csikszentmihalyi, M. (2016) 'Teamwork and flow proneness mitigate the negative effect of excess challenge on flow state', *The Journal of Positive Psychology*, 12 (3): 284–89.

Vansteenkiste, M., Lens, W. and Deci, E.L. (2006) 'Intrinsic versus extrinsic goal contents in self-determination theory: Another look at the quality of academic motivation', *Educational Psychologist*, 41 (1): 19–31.

Watt, H.M.G. and Richardson, P.W. (2007) 'Motivational factors influencing teaching as a career choice: Development and validation of the FIT-Choice Scale', *Journal of Experimental Education*, 75 (3): 167–202.

Watt, H.M.G. and Richardson, P.W. (2008) 'Motivations, perceptions, and aspirations concerning teaching as a career for different types of beginning teachers', *Learning and Instruction*, 18 (3): 408–28.

Watt, H.M.G. et al. (2012) 'Motivations for choosing teaching as a career: An international comparison using the FIT-Choice scale', *Teaching and Teacher Education*, 28 (6): 791–805.

3

INTRINSIC AND EXTRINSIC MOTIVATION

Chapter guide

In this chapter, you will learn about:

- Traditional views of motivation

- Intrinsic motivation: Self-actualisation, autonomy and connectedness

- Self-determination and self-regulation for pupils and teachers

- Extrinsic motivation: A balanced view

In recent years, educators have questioned old orthodoxies in teaching: the value of rewards and different forms of motivation. Some of these views have been extreme. There have been suggestions that some rewards can be detrimental to long-term pupil well-being (Palmer, 2015). We do not take an extreme position here, but we question the nature of motivation and how it is analysed in the school setting. What is motivating for pupils and teachers? Is this a constant feature in the classroom and the lives of pupils and teachers, or is this dynamic, changing at different stages of a child's learning and a teacher's career? Recent work on intrinsic motivation highlights personal growth, connectedness and autonomy as central to a sense of intrinsic motivation. We explore this in the case of teachers and pupils, recognising that the lines between intrinsic and extrinsic motivation are blurred. We believe that education built on strong values, which sets out ultimately to empower learners, can, indeed, change attitudes towards learning in both pupils and teachers. Case studies from both primary and secondary schools are explored in this chapter. In particular, we are interested in motivation from the point of view of the child and the teacher. What teachers think is motivating for children is not the same as children's own ideas of what is motivating.

Immersing learners in genuinely inspiring activities is the nearest we will come to Csikszentmihalyi's (1990) concept of flow in education. Curiosity for learning, in which learners of all ages are challenged to learn about themselves, others and the world around them, is our objective. To this extent, the love of learning and the joy of learning is our ultimate objective. As Dewey stated, 'Education is its own reward!'.

Traditional views of motivation

As always in education, language can obscure the way we see different concepts. Zimmerman and Schunk (2008) analyse the historical development of motivation. They explain that the term 'motivation' comes from the Latin 'movere' to move. This is interesting as we often conceive of motivation as something that might both physically and emotionally move us. To bring this back to an educational context, they define motivation as an activity focused on achieving a goal in a sustained way (Zimmerman and Schunk, 2008). That motivation is 'goal-directed' is very important in education. It could be a 'knowledge-based goal' – to learn something new, like different ways to represent fractions in a primary school; or how to do something, like how to play the guitar. It could be social, working with your friends in schools on a project, which cements friendship. Or it could even be moral and ethical – a faith-based school may want children and young people to demonstrate certain moral and ethical behaviours, to which pupils are happy to aspire or even conform.

Motivation has never been a clear subject. Zimmerman and Schunk (2008) describe the historical development of the concept of motivation. Motivation has often been seen as being synonymous with terms like 'volition' and 'will'. It is far beyond the scope of this book to explain these dimensions. By the mid-twentieth century, different traditions were emerging. The cognitive tradition saw motivation as a process: less an observable response to external factors and more an internal process. Maslow (1954) sees motivation more holistically. Individual responses to events are always an attempt to maintain balance amongst beliefs, attitudes, opinions and values. So in a way, the cognitivists see that each of us has a theory of motivation that guides our activities. In school, different motivational theories compete for acceptance. Humanistic theories, such as that of Maslow, are often associated with the work of Rogers (1963). Humanists see human beings as having choices and seek to control their lives as much as possible. Motivation in humanistic terms is about capabilities and potentials. Striving to choose activities, which are seen as fulfilling, enhancing or affirming of individuals, is the core of all analyses of motivation. In Maslow's (1954) view, the ultimate 'need' is for self-actualisation, or personal growth.

Traces of the above theories of motivation can be seen in approaches to motivation in current forms of education. For instance, some schools in England still have a framework for behaviour management built on the idea of learners' responses to external stimuli (rewards and sanctions) ruling their behaviour. This could be seen as a behaviourist conception of motivation, whereas other schools see the role of self-regulation of behaviour as an interaction of learner beliefs, values and family contexts. Behavioural rules are often agreed between pupils and their teachers, with the ultimate goal of passing control to the learner to self-regulate their behaviour because this is the right thing to do. In this case, motivation is the process underpinning the goal of good behaviour in school: a more cognitive and humanistic approach to motivation. This can be seen as a process of control – initially by the teacher and eventually by the pupil. This somewhat mirrors the process of internalising social routines and rules, explained by the zone of proximal development in the social constructivist theory of Vygotsky (1978).

Before we move on to talk about different aspects of motivation, it is important to reflect on your own theories in this area.

REFLECTION POINT

Consider your own theories of motivation for school learning:

- Do you see the learner as a passive responder to the school environment?
- Is the aim of learning ultimately to transfer control and responsibility for many aspects of the school experience to the learning?
- Can you see traits of a behavioural, cognitivist, humanistic or even Freudian theories in your own views of motivation in your own practices?
- How do learners in your classes see themselves, in the above terms?
- Are your views of what motivates pupils and young people different from their views of what motivates them?
- How does your school policy and practice encapsulate motivation?

There may be an aspiration to develop self-controlled learners, but the gap between values and practice might be quite significant – for pupils, teachers and the school more generally.

To paint a picture of the ideal classroom, the authors would emphasise the role of values, beliefs and the degree to which learners exercise self-regulation in class. Here, we are not just talking about blind compliance to meet behavioural expectations, but about exploring how learners see themselves. One mathematics professor said that using a chalkboard to teach was important in a university maths department so that students learn what it means to become mathematicians, rather than just learning mathematics skills. Apparently, mathematicians have a preference for teaching with chalkboard as opposed to pens and whiteboards when teaching a class. We subscribe to the view that education is as much about the person you become as about the knowledge that you gain. Teaching maths is as much about learning how to think and be a mathematician as it is about developing mathematical knowledge. We also think that values and beliefs around learning in school are critical not only for motivational purposes, but also because they are central to the content of teaching and learning in any subject. To that extent, we recognise the influence of humanism as a motivational theory on our own practices.

Zimmerman and Schunk (2008) clearly see a cognitivist approach to motivation to be more compelling. Seeing the learner as a self-regulator with a theory that drives their motivation in school is central to the work of Dweck (Elliot and Dweck, 2013). Dweck's influence on school learning and theories of motivation has been huge in the first part of the twenty-first century in schools in the UK. Often, in the areas of 'resilience' and so-called 'growth mindset', the so-called 'self-theories' of Carol Dweck have been referred to by educationalists and school leaders. This certainly touches on motivation, learning and teaching in schools and is therefore worthy of some discussion. What is more, Dweck's framework helps us to reinforce the essential purpose of education – the nature of teaching, learning and the distinctive characteristics of the learner ensuing from the school system. To this, we would add the characteristic experience of the learning process. Both outcomes and experience are important in primary and secondary schools. Amazing test and exam results are not justified by tedious and instrumental approaches to teaching in classes of demotivated learners.

Leading on from socio-cognitivists like Albert Bandura, it could be a 'knowledge-based goal' – to learn something new: like different ways to represent fractions in a primary school; or how to do something, such as how to play the guitar. It could be social, working with your friends in school on a project, which cements friendship. Or, it could even be moral and ethical – a faith-based school may want children and young people to demonstrate certain moral and ethical behaviours, to which pupils are happy to aspire or even conform.

Dweck thought that learners, and by implication schools, placed too much emphasis on the completion of learning activities rather than the actual learning. Allied to this, learners often received praise for attainment and achievement rather than for the effort they put into an activity. Dweck's view is that many learners with a performance orientation to learning have a fixed view of intelligence: 'we are born with a certain level of intelligence and we cannot do anything to change this' (2014: 1–2). However, those with a mastery view of learning recognise that intelligence is not fixed, and that putting in more effort to an activity will result in greater learning progress. This is where the term 'growth mindset' comes from. These individuals have an approach that emphasises the potential to impact on your learning and develop intelligence: in short, to grow as learners. Of course, effort on its own will not result in progress. Good teaching and a conducive learning environment do make a difference. But, when the learner believes that by working harder in an area they can thereby improve their learning, it does make a difference to their mindset and potential to achieve in the long term.

In classes, we see the impact of Dweck's theories of motivation and learning. Overly praising intelligence emphasises that the learner is set at a certain level, whereas emphasising praise for the learners' effort reinforces the learners' view of themselves as being mastery learners, capable of even higher outcomes. Elliot and Dweck (2013) make the same claims about the importance of process as opposed to person-focused feedback. Dweck's research showed that learners given more process feedback ('You worked really hard on that') were more capable of persisting in the face of obstacles and were more resilient than those being given more person-centred feedback ('You're really smart at maths'). These elements will be further discussed in relation to both pupils and teachers. But it is important to recognise Dweck's considerable contribution here. She has managed to make a theoretical and professional link between the emotional aspects of motivation and the cognitive aspects of learning through a socio-cognitivist perspective of learning. Further developing a cognitivist view, she manages to link together emotional, social and cognitivist aspects of learning in a theory of learning and motivation. As stated, this has implications both for the teacher (how we praise the learner) and for the learner (the very goals of education should be mastery, not performance of understanding). One of the critical distinctions in the literature is that between intrinsic and extrinsic motivation.

Intrinsic motivation

What are the antecedents of 'intrinsic motivation'? 'Effectance motivation' was coined by White (1959) to explain the feelings of motivation associated with mastery of a skill or activity early in life. Having mastered a simple task, a baby or toddler would have a feeling of personal mastery or efficacy. This is seen to have an important evolutionary function, as it helps people deal competently with environmental factors. Moving towards a more cognitive explanation of intrinsic motivation enabled an analysis of the internal cognitive structures, which resulted in motivation for an activity or learning for its own sake. Zimmerman and Schunk identify four factors that encourage intrinsic motivation:

Challenge: Feeling motivated to complete activities that are in themselves challenging but that are within the competence of the learner.

Curiosity: Feeling good about completing a strange or incongruous activity, which enables growth of understanding.

Control: Feeling able to choose and have control over learning.

Fantasy: Focusing attention through a fantasy or game-based activity.

Intrinsic motivation is a factor of the context. As an individual, we may experience a sense of challenge differently from another person. What is intrinsically motivating for one person may not be for another. It is true to say as well that levels of intrinsic motivation may rise or fall over a period of time. Just because something is intrinsically motivating for you as a child is no guarantee that you will have the same intrinsic motivation later in on life. It is also quite logical that someone can be both intrinsically motivated and extrinsically motivated for an activity. For instance, a pupil in school may love reading Charles Dickens as an activity in itself, whilst also aspiring to achieve a high grade at the end of year exam in English because this will allow them to pass to the next stage of the school system at the age of 16 years.

Learners can have different things they are interested in. We can have an interest in an activity like reading, but this is no guarantee that it is intrinsically motivating in itself. Logically, but unlikely, is the possibility that someone may be intrinsically motivated but have no interest in something. It is possible, for instance, that someone may be motivated to sit exams without having an interest in exams. It is, however, counter-intuitive.

Bound up in the concept of intrinsic motivation is the idea of 'interest'. Zimmerman and Schunk (2008) define this as how much someone likes or is engaged in an activity. Interest can be looked at in different ways. Broadly, we can categorise this in two main ways – internal or personal and external or situational forms of interest:

Internal or personal interest is our liking for certain topics, pursuits or areas of learning. A child might love learning about dinosaurs. One teacher recounts the tale of a 6-year-old pupil she taught. They did a simple project on fossils. His mum later said that he was so interested in this topic, that it became a lifelong interest. He studied this at the age of 16 in geology, studied palaeontology at university and is now a worldwide expert on fossils. This all started with a project in infant school. Now it has become a lifelong interest . . . or even obsession. Personal interest can develop at quite an early age and is relatively stable across our life span. That does not mean that personal interests at the age of 5 are always with us for life. But there is clearly a link between early experiences, opportunities and interests – how many musicians have a friend, relative or teacher to thank for introducing them to music and the playing of a musical instrument? Of course, such personal interests can develop at the age of 5 or 55. For both young people and teachers, this is an optimistic point – everyone can develop a personal interest at some point in their lives. We also need to recognise that what interests an adult does not necessarily interest a child. Two people can have a personal interest in music, but one might love Bach and the other might love Bowie. Giving children and adults a broad range of learning experiences provides everyone with the opportunity to find their 'thing'. This is an argument for a broad and balanced school curriculum for children as well as a broad and balanced professional development curriculum for children.

External or situational interest is the degree to which we are engaged and like the activities or the way the task is presented. These are the contextual factors outside the individual that provide interest. We may not particularly like French as a school subject, but the opportunity to take part in a language simulation activity may provide real interest for a learner and their teacher. Often, cooperative forms of learning, like jigsaw learning, envoy groups and snowballing activities, are reported by both pupils and teachers as being interesting because of the way they are carried out. One such lesson involved a group of 10-year-old primary pupils learning about different types of bridges. A trainee teacher had planned this lesson around some resource packs distributed to several groups in the class. Each group was given information about a type of bridge. They had to find out about the various characteristics of the bridge in their base group. They then worked in groups to explain their 'bridge' to one person from each of the other groups (an envoy activity). This all happened on a Friday afternoon, in a subject area (geography) for which the children had so far shown little interest. This was an amazing lesson, quite edgy for the trainee teacher, as she did not have complete confidence in this type of teaching, but also clearly quite different for the children. They absolutely loved this lesson. All of them explained that they really enjoyed learning like this. It caught their interest to start with, gaining their attention with the novelty of the teaching approach. It maintained their interest because it was purposeful and meaningful, with the opportunity for the learner to maintain a good degree of control over the learning (speed of delivery, use of language and manipulation of concrete materials). Catching and maintaining interest are important variables in situational interest. Of course, as in the fossil project example, what starts as an interesting activity (situational interest) can make a topic interesting over the longer term (personal interest).

We would also like to identify a third aspect of interest, which we would see as being internal to the individual. Several theorists talk about interest as a psychological state (Zimmerman and Schunk, 2008). Here, they explain that the value that the learner has for a topic will impact on their interest. Even where there is low knowledge, a topic that is highly valued will generate interest, but a topic that is not valued will not generate interest. We would also identify some learners who are just really interested in learning. They not only value certain topics, but they value learning more generally. These learners have a genuine curiosity for learning and life. Is it not the role of all teachers to develop a love of learning in their learners? Is it not the role of all head teachers and school leaders to develop a love of learning in their staff?

REFLECTION POINT

- What do your pupils find interesting in school?
- What do you find interesting in school?

Copy out and complete Table 3.1 and Table 3.2 in order to identify preferences. You could talk to individual learners or groups of learners in your class to identify personal and situational interests.

Table 3.1   Interests of pupils

The child and young person	Example
1. Topics in school that interest me	School subjects, other school learning, like music lessons, sports clubs and other clubs
2. Topics outside of school that interest me	Issues in society, television, social media, reading, hobbies and other clubs

---

The child and young person	Example
3. Activities and other ways of working in school that interest me	Learning in groups, learning outside, going on school trips, talking to invited speakers
4. Activities and ways of working in class that do not interest me	Learning by repetition and rote for some people is not motivating.

Table 3.2 Interests of teachers

The adult and professional in school	Example
1. Topics in school that interest me as a teacher	School subject teaching, extracurricular clubs and extracurricular learning
2. Topics outside of school that interest me	Issues in society, family, television, social media, reading, hobbies and other clubs
3. Activities and other ways of working in school that interest me	Learning in groups, learning outside, going on school trips, talking to invited speakers
4. Activities and ways of working in class that do not interest me	Developing the curriculum through large group meetings, where there is insufficient opportunity to discuss the issues.

Once you and the pupils have answered the above questions, take some time to compare and contrast your interests. You could plot the two approaches to interest in both school learning and interests outside of school, in the Venn diagram in Figure 3.1. The teacher's and learner's personal and situational interests can then be compared.

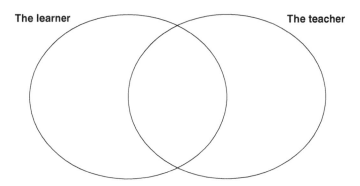

The learner   The teacher

Figure 3.1 Personal and situational interests of school learning

This is a really useful activity to complete. You might be interested in nineteenth-century literature, but your Year 5 class might be more interested

(Continued)

(Continued)

in *Harry Potter* by J.K. Rowling (1997–2007) at the moment. Your Year 9 class might love reading *The Machine Gunners* by Robert Westall (1975), but the National Curriculum might require you to teach *Tom's Midnight Garden* by Phillipa Pearce (1958).

It can, however, be very powerful to share your own preferences for learning with the class and vice versa. Learners love a passionate and interesting teacher.

You might see some aspects of interest that link to motivation. Personal and situational interests all look like they could be reminiscent of intrinsic motivation. Having a personal interest or liking a way we learn could be interpreted as being learning for its own sake. Playing a musical instrument or working in novel learning activities can be motivating for its own sake. It could also be that the longer-term gains for an interest or way of learning could be a driving force. Practising scales in music can be a fantastically pleasurable thing, for some people. But it also can be seen as a means to a long-term goal like passing a music grade exam. Again, according to the individual, passing a music grade may be pleasurable in itself, but it also might be a requirement for entry to music college. The reward for practising your scales might ultimately be entry to music college.

Extrinsic motivation

Extrinsic motivation can be present alongside intrinsic motivation and personal and situational interest. It is a question of degree: How much does this influence the learner and the teacher in the classroom? Extrinsic motivation is commonly defined as motivation to take part in or complete an activity as a means to an end. Extrinsic motivation is often associated with the concept of 'reward': a later or deferred positive experience some time after the original activity. In class, an extrinsic motivation might be seen as a kind of implied learning contract: if you complete this activity and you achieve this learning outcome, then I will give you this reward; I will tell you what you have to learn and these are the success criteria by which I/we will judge whether you are entitled to the agreed reward. The reward might be physical (a sticker or stamp in your book), social (celebrating your success in front of the class or school), emotional (a teacher or parent expressing pride in the learner's success) or even monetary (the reward for both learners and their teacher might be a financial gift from parent to child or a financial bonus from school to teacher). Of course, a reward for a younger learner may not work for an older learner. Many children in English schools would find it incredibly embarrassing to celebrate their successes in front of the class – for some classes and schools, it is not cool to learn. In other schools, it is clear that a genuine love of learning is at the heart of the school for both adult and younger learners. Rewarding a love of learning and positive learning attitudes as well as specific learning outcomes can be a very powerful approach.

CASE STUDY

A primary school in Kent believes in every child's ability to realise their potential. No different from most schools, you would say. But, the head and senior staff in the school have a real commitment to developing every child as an individual. In the school entrance there is a big display of the experiences that every child will access by the end of their seven years in the school. From taking part in a Shakespeare play in the school's outside stage to weekly learning in the school forest, children have an incredibly varied set of experiences. From these experiences, many develop personal interests that are sustained throughout their lives. It is clear to see how personal interests develop in such a positive and colourful learning environment.

Situational interests are sustained by a range of learning settings (inside and outside the school) and a range of teaching methods (Mrs Wellings' online spellings come to mind), and with a progression throughout the school. Every class emphasises certain learning dispositions that build up, using different languages from the early to the later years. Importantly, this is not merely management speak that is not justified by the actual practices of the classroom. Even at a young age, children are able to articulate how they learn and how the learning dispositions help them to achieve a growth mindset.

Talking to both pupils and teachers, it is clear to see how they are motivated for learning in school for itself and also for what it leads to. The school does very well in external inspections, but it also achieves well in pupil and parent evaluations of the school learning experience.

This is a school that develops interest and motivation in both children and adults.

It is very interesting from the example in the case study above that pupils and staff are all engaged in developing interest and motivation in school. Pupils are encouraged to be self-regulating learners, recognising that they can exert control over their learning. That the individual can exercise control and influence their learning is obviously an underpinning principle in the work of Carol Dweck.

Personal control and motivation

In the early 1960s, Rotter (1966) identified a very interesting role of the self in learning. His social learning theory focused on the role of beliefs in the degree of control an individual could exercise over their learning. In fact, the set of beliefs became, for the individual, something of a generalised set of beliefs about successful and unsuccessful learning. Depending on their views, a person could be seen to have an 'internal locus of control': the individual feels that they can influence outcomes of learning. The people tend to have a more intrinsic approach to motivation and mastery learning since they believe that they can influence the outcomes of learning by their own efforts. On the other hand, those with an 'external locus of control' tend to see themselves as more recipients and victims of events, rather than being able to influence them. They have a tendency to see effort as worthless in learning, since they will not be able to impact on their learning. On a practical level, this could explain why some learners in school (or, indeed, university) are more passive, less motivated learners, apt to blame other people for their own failures to achieve learning and understanding in an activity. Other learners seem to be more willing to tackle tasks that might be seen as challenging. Where things do not work out, those with an internal locus of control seem to bounce back, with a good attitude to learning. Zimmerman and Schunk (2008) identify a number of implications for teachers and learners in personal responsibility for learning.

CASE STUDY

A secondary academy has worked hard to put the work of Zimmerman and Schunk (2008) into practice. In order to foster personal responsibility in learning, they suggest the following key steps:

Model personal responsibility and believe that you can develop it in students: Teachers who take care in organising their teaching *show* their students good learning practices, rather than just telling them. Isobel, Head of English, has worked hard to empower her staff to take ownership of new developments in the English curriculum. This has been an important factor in showing students that teachers have responsibilities and that they will always exercise these in a proactive and professional way: you can't expect students to take responsibility if teachers won't do that.

Provide students with options to choose from and have them consider the consequences of each choice: Good practice in the early years suggests that teachers should not put out all the materials needed for a task. Children should make choices in the materials and equipment they need for a task. This makes them more empowered learners. A good example is the role of students in contributing to the different approaches to learning in school. They identify a range of learning strategies that students believe make a difference to their learning. They provide options for teachers to give students different activities in class. Project-based learning is now seen as a very good way to give students choices in how and what they learn.

Foster internal attributions – do not allow students to blame others for their failures or attribute success to luck: A blame culture is the default position for some students. Getting them to realise that it is what they do that makes a difference in learning is a challenge, especially for a school that had developed quite a blame culture from senior managers to students in the past. A new head teacher challenged this approach. Slowly but surely, the culture of blame is being replaced by a 'can do' approach to teaching and learning in both teachers and students.

Have students set goals, periodically evaluate their progress and decide whether a change in strategy is necessary: Helping students to set goals makes the learning more personal and aligns activities more with the students' own interests. It gives them more ownership. An assertive mentoring approach helps students to set their own targets, which a learning mentor will discuss termly with students. Results in end-of-year exams are going up for 16- and 18-year-olds, alongside student and parent evaluations of the student learning experience.

These practical solutions can be seen in many recent approaches to school development, for example in approaches to 'growth mindset'. Underpinning the approach to motivation in this area is 'self-determination theory' (Deci and Ryan, 2008). Deci and Ryan's work has been incredibly influential in the area of motivation and how this translates to teaching and learning in school. Schools would do well to consider the implications of this work.

Self-determination and extrinsic motivation

The great progress made by Deci and Ryan (2008) was in their analysis of motivation. No longer is motivation seen as a binary concept of intrinsic and extrinsic motivation. They saw motivation as a continuum from no motivation at all through to entirely internal factors that motivate the learner intrinsically. The great development was to analyse differences in forms of regulation which impact on extrinsic motivation.

Classically, we might recognise extrinsic motivation as being through 'extrinsic regulation', in which the learner is subject to rewards and sanctions as an act of compliance. An everyday analysis of extrinsic motivation may well see learners' and teachers' responses in school as an act of compliance, subject to a variety of physical, emotional, social and cognitive rewards and sanctions.

As a process, we can see that there are subtleties in the way that extrinsic motivation can interact with the self. Whilst the individual learner may not immediately engage with the focus for learning, there may be a movement away from seeking recognition from others as well as starting to take pride in one's own successes. This, Deci and Ryan (2008) call 'introjection'. Critically, reward and sanction are moving from an external to an internal mechanism.

As the value attributed to an activity moves from an external to an internal origin, goals and motivation become 'self-endorsed'. This stage of extrinsic motivation is called 'identification'. Whilst there may still be some differences between external factors that motivate the learner, and their own view of the activities, there is a growing meeting of perspectives of the self and those around them. A school might identify a mastery approach to learning as being important, but a student might still focus on performance of understanding. University tutors often cite undergraduate students as being very instrumental in their learning, but soon becoming accustomed to and adopting a more mastery-focused approach to learning. This could be seen as a movement from externally regulated motivation towards more internally focused forms of intrinsic motivation.

The last stage before intrinsic motivation is 'integration'. At this point, goals are aligned with those formerly managed externally. Importantly, the learner integrates both internal and external sources of information that impact on motivation. It is not fully intrinsic motivation as the origins of the motivation are not entirely self-driven and originating from the self.

If intrinsic motivation is the end result of a process of internalisation, then there are very interesting socio-cognitive parallels with the zone of proximal development, according to Vygotsky (1978). His assertion that 'everything that exists on the psychological plane, first existed on the sociological plane' mirrors the analysis of Deci and Ryan (2008). Whilst intrinsic motivation can have its origins from within the individual, seeing motivation as 'emergent' recognises the changing and transformative nature of motivation from external to internal through a process of socialisation. For schools, we can say that motivation and the process by which intrinsic motivation develops is in turn a process by which schools can support, teach and influence motivation in their pupils. A broad and balanced curriculum should therefore not only plan for the cognitive dimensions of learning, but it should also consider planning for the process of emergent motivation.

Chapter summary

- Education built on strong values, which sets out ultimately to empower learners, can indeed change attitudes towards learning in both pupils and teachers.
- Motivation is 'a process whereby goal-directed activity is instigated and sustained' (Zimmerman and Schunk, 2008).
- Zimmerman and Schunk (ibid.) identify 'challenge', 'curiosity', 'control' and 'fantasy' as supporting motivation.
- Dweck's view is that many learners with a performance orientation to learning have a fixed view of intelligence.
- Depending on their views, a person could be seen to have an 'internal locus of control'.
- Those with an 'external locus of control' tend to see themselves as more recipients and victims of events, rather than being able to influence them.
- 'Personal interest' is our liking for certain topics, pursuits or areas of learning.
- 'Situational interest' is the degree to which we are engaged and like the activities or the way the task is presented.
- 'Extrinsic motivation' is commonly defined as motivation to take part in or complete an activity as a means to an end. Extrinsic motivation is often associated with the concept of 'reward': a later or deferred positive experience, some time after the original activity.
- Whilst the individual learner may not immediately engage with the focus for learning, there may be a movement away from seeking recognition from others as well as starting to take pride in one's own successes. This, Deci and Ryan (2008) call 'introjection'. Critically, reward and sanction are moving from an external to an internal mechanism.
- As the value attributed to an activity moves from an external to an internal origin, goals and motivation become 'self-endorsed'. This stage of extrinsic motivation is called 'identification'.
- The last stage before intrinsic motivation is 'integration'. At this point, goals are aligned with those formerly managed externally.
- Whilst intrinsic motivation can have its origins from within the individual, seeing motivation as 'emergent' recognises the changing and

transformative nature of motivation from external to internal through a process of socialisation. For schools, we can say that motivation and the process by which intrinsic motivation develops is a process by which schools can support, teach and influence motivation in their pupils.

Further reading

Deci, E.L., Ryan, R.M. (2008) 'Facilitating optimal motivation and psychological well-being across life's domains', *Canadian Psychology*, *49* (1): 14–23.
This explains self-determination theory and is particularly relevant for understanding motivation and the factors in learning that encourage well-being.

Dweck, C.S. (2000) *Self-Theories: Their Role in Motivation, Personality, and Development*. New York: Psychology Press.
The author explains the basis of her theories of learning, linking motivation and approaches to learning. In our opinion, one of the best books written in this area; and it is highly accessible.

Zimmerman, B.J. and Schunk, D.H. (2008) 'Motivation: An essential dimension of self-regulated learning', in D.H. Schunk and B.J. Zimmerman (eds), *Motivation and Self-Regulated Learning: Theory, Research, and Applications*. Mahwah, NJ: Lawrence Erlbaum Associates Publishers.
Self-determination is a central concept in learning. This text explains in a very accessible way what this means and why it is important.

Bibliography

Csikszentmihalyi, M. (1990) 'The domain of creativity', in M.A. Runco and R.S. Albert (eds), *Theories of Creativity*. Newbury Park, CA: Sage.

Deci, E.L. and Ryan, R.M. (2008) 'Facilitating optimal motivation and psychological well-being across life's domains', *Canadian Psychology*, *49* (1): 14–23.

Dweck, C.S. (2014) Mindsets and math/science achievement. Available at: http://www.growthmindsetmaths.com/.../mindset_and_math_science_achievement_-_nov_2... (accessed May 2018).

Elliot, A.J. and Dweck, C.S. (eds) (2013) *Handbook of Competence and Motivation*. New York and London: Guilford Press.

Maslow, A.H. (1954) 'The instinctoid nature of basic needs', *Journal of Personality*, *22*: 326–47.

Palmer, S. (2015) *Toxic Childhood: How the Modern World is Damaging Our Children and What We Can Do About It*. London: Orion.

Pearce, P. (1958) *Tom's Midnight Garden*. Oxford: Oxford University Press.

Rogers, C.R. (1963) 'Toward a science of the person', *Journal of Humanistic Psychology*, *3* (2): 72–92.

Rotter, J.B. (1966) 'Generalized expectancies for internal versus external control of reinforcement', *Psychological Monographs: General and Applied*, *80* (1): 1–28.

Rowling, J.K. (1997–2007) *Harry Potter, series*. London: Bloomsbury.

Vygotsky, L.S. (1978) *Mind in Society: The Development of Higher Psychological Process*. Cambridge, MA: Harvard University Press.

Westall, R. (1975) *The Machine Gunners*. London: Macmillan Children's Books.

White, R. (1959) Motivation reconsidered: The concept of competence. *Psychological Review*, *66*: 297–333.

Zimmerman, B.J. and Schunk, D.H. (2008) 'Motivation: An essential dimension of self-regulated learning', in D.H. Schunk and B.J. Zimmerman (eds), *Motivation and Self-Regulated Learning: Theory, Research, and Applications*. Mahwah, NJ: Lawrence Erlbaum Associates Publishers.

4

BETTER LEARNING, BETTER BEHAVIOUR

Chapter guide

In this chapter, you will learn about:

- The influence of the relationship between teacher and learner on classroom behaviour

- The importance of modelling positive behaviours and the key steps that help to make modelling work in practice

- The importance of praise and how an understanding of core qualities can be applied to encourage positive classroom environments

- Practical ways of dealing with negative behaviours without compromising the positivity of your classroom ethos

- The importance of positivity on a wider level with colleagues and within your broader context

---

REFLECTION POINT

- What are your values and beliefs surrounding the behaviour of learners?
- What behaviours do you want learners to adopt in your classroom and why?
- How can you share your values with learners?
- Do your classroom routines and behaviour management expectations fit with your values?

Managing behaviour is one of the key concerns of many teachers, both early on and later in their careers. In fact, when you take a step back in order to reflect on the nature of classroom behaviour, it seems almost absurd that 30 or so learners, whether energetic, overexcited primary school children or potentially surly, confrontational teenagers, generally cooperate with the whims and caprices of their teacher, who is often in the minority as the only adult in the room. Why do most children cooperate most of the time? Is there intrinsic authority in the status of the teacher? Does the wider power of the school system bestow greater authority on the teacher as its in-classroom representative? Possibly. However, in most classrooms, where the atmosphere is positive, cooperative and purposeful, this is rooted in a shared value system and a collaborative effort to strive for the best possible experience. It is not enough to simply force cooperation through threats or coercion. The teacher needs to move from just managing behaviour to inspiring positive behaviour, with learners actively choosing to be participatory members of the learning environment and exercising their own agency in their choice to make positive decisions regarding behaviour.

The best behaviour management systems do not manage behaviour at all, but rather, are evident when the teacher and students are united as equal participants on a journey to their shared goal of educational and personal development. Nurmi found that 'students' academic performance was negatively associated with conflict . . . and positively with closeness' (2012: 191) in a meta-analysis of 19 studies. Similarly, Cornelius-White concluded from a meta-analysis of 119 studies (from 1948 to 2004) that 'positive relationships, nondirectivity, empathy, warmth, and encouraging thinking and learning are the specific teacher variables that are above average [in their effect on positive student outcomes] compared with other educational innovation' (2007: 134). Nurmi, like Cornelius-White – whose study focused on analysing empirical evidence in order to support or refute the ideas of the person-centred learning at the heart of 'classical, humanistic education and today's constructivist learner-centered model' (2012: 113) – also emphasised the importance of the learner's role in this relationship, concluding that 'students' characteristics may play an important role in the kinds of relationships teachers build with individual students' (2007: 195). From this perspective, the student is as supportive of the teacher's development as the teacher is of theirs.

In order to achieve this equal agency, however, learners must be motivated and ultimately empowered. This means that learners must have the choice of whether to cooperate or not. The teacher can influence them, as can their peer group, but they must also embrace the risks as well as the benefits involved in transferring choice, agency and responsibility to their learners. If behaviour is managed too tightly by the teacher, students are not given the opportunity to self-regulate and internalise the expectations of wider social environments. In this instance, a teacher, at best, can only motivate their learners, encouraging them to conform to the rules of the classroom and to cooperate in the learning experience through exercising the teacher's own individual authority. Ironically, the learners can still reject this environment and its managerial teaching style, so the risk of empowering learners and giving them the opportunity to exercise their own authority in a safe and supportive setting is a risk that exists in any classroom, and therefore should not dissuade teachers from moving towards a behaviour model that focuses on empowerment rather than passive cooperation and adherence to rules.

Putting it into practice

How, then, can we, as teachers, apply these principles surrounding the engagement, motivation and empowerment of learners to the promotion of positive behaviours in learning environments? The relationship between teacher and learner is not unilateral but bilateral and reciprocal, with each interaction shaping and developing the values and identity of all the participants. Far from viewing learners as passive conduits of knowledge who must be controlled, we can collaboratively establish and sustain a cooperative and inspiring learning environment through valuing their perspectives, autonomy and agency within our teaching. So, what does this look like in practice? Do we envisage a slightly dazed teacher, beatific smile on their face as they survey a classroom full of anarchic children, all exercising their autonomy and agency as loudly and chaotically as possible? Hopefully not. Autonomy and agency are not the same as anarchy and rebellion. Learners still need to be aware of the expectations of their learning environment and the boundaries that are in place; however, these boundaries must be firmly rooted and clearly explained in light of the shared values of that equal, bilateral learning environment. It is not enough to reprimand Jimmy for talking over another student because it is a school rule. This teaches Jimmy nothing. In fact, if Jimmy is not the only student talking but perhaps the individual chosen by the teacher in order to reinforce a rule to the whole class, then Jimmy has learned that he is a scapegoat for others and that his teacher unfairly discriminates against him. He feels angered, embittered and disempowered. However, if Jimmy is told that he needs to stop talking because the views of everyone in the class are important and he needs to be respectful towards them in order to, in turn, merit their respect, then he has learned that this is the central tenet of the classroom environment. Jimmy may still reject the verbal reminder, but, if he does so, he is also choosing to reject the values of the classroom environment and the ethos that the rest of the class are seeking to uphold. He forces himself outside of the group not because he has disobeyed you as the teacher, but because he has infringed on the rights of his peers.

The impact of the relationship between teacher and student is significant when considering behaviour. Gregory and Ripski (2008) found that teachers who valued relationships with students were more likely to be trusted by their learners and perceived as reasonable and fair authority figures. Here, the direct correlation between the teacher's professed values and the students' perceptions of them suggests that the teacher's individual vision is communicated to their students through classroom interactions. The communication of these values can be seen as taking place on a daily basis, with the students unconsciously identifying the values of the teacher through their actions within the learning environment. Kuczynski's bidirectional model, which emphasises the importance of both teacher and learner as equal participants in their relationship, emphasises that 'a relationship is formed between two partners as they accumulate a history of interactions and begin to interject symbolic representations or expectancies of their past interactions in to subsequent interactions with each other' (2003: 8).

In the case of teacher–learner relationships, the positivity or negativity of these interactions leads to the relationship being functional or dysfunctional, with the behaviour of both learners and teachers adjusting accordingly. This places a serious responsibility on teachers as each interaction clearly impacts upon the quality of the overall relationship between teacher and learner. A negative interaction, perhaps caused by external factors such as tiredness, an unpleasant meeting that morning or any other depressing or aggravating event, can therefore be incredibly damaging. This does not mean that, in order to establish a positive classroom ethos, teachers need to polish their angelic halos and take a deep breath, but that teachers need to acknowledge that if their actions and attitudes can be impacted upon by external events, then so, too, can a student's. If teachers and students can objectively reflect on the impact of these external factors, then they can allow each other the space to react to them, positively or negatively. The teacher who shouts at the class as a knee-jerk reaction to having overslept and been in a rush all morning, for example, loses the respect of the learners as the learners' roles within the classroom have been devalued. They move from being active participants in the learning environment to being perceived as a potentially unsolvable source of unhappiness to the teacher. The teacher who explains to the class that they have had a difficult day and want to apologise in advance in case they are a little snappy compared to usual, immediately shows that they value their relationship with their learners. They have not lost face or authority in the eyes of their learners (but they will lose lesson time if they give in and respond to the students' sympathetic questions).

There is clear evidence of the benefits of a positive classroom culture and the establishment and maintenance of positive relationships between teacher and learners. We now turn to the practicalities of establishing positive relationships in the classroom.

Establishing positive interactions

Within any learning environment, it is important to value learners' identities. Use their names to show that you know them as individuals rather than as a homogeneous group of learners. Get to know their interests and link up to these in both your planning and your interaction with the learners. Personalisation of learning should not just refer to planning specifically for the perceived ability level of a learner, but rather to the way that the teacher mediates the content knowledge they aim to deliver or the skills they wish to develop in the learner, tailoring this learning to their interests as far as possible.

It is important to note that we are not advocating that teachers spend hours and hours of curriculum time on social aims, but rather, we are encouraging teachers to approach their learners with curiosity and a high level of interest in every lesson. Far from demanding that all learners write a paragraph about, for example, their family at the start of each term, we encourage you to listen carefully to your learners and build up a picture of their identities and experiences, which you can then refer back to in order to establish positive interactions, rooted in understanding, familiarity and shared experiences.

Alongside personalisation of learning, praise is an important way of establishing a positive tone and incentivising desirable learning behaviours. However, praise can be both difficult to give and sometimes even more difficult to receive. How many of us squirm when one of our core qualities is identified and celebrated? Is this because we are fearful of others being able to recognise our traits so easily? Are we scarred by some half-remembered, negative childhood experiences of praise? Even if we are uncomfortable with praise, we need to get to grips with the impact that it can have on a classroom environment. As is often the case in teaching, encouraging praise starts with you. As a teacher, you have opportunities throughout the day to give feedback on learners' attitudes, effort levels and performance. If your feedback is limited to only signposting improvements that the learner needs to make, then there is no recognition of the efforts they have made in order to reach their current stage of the learning process. Even those of us who find it difficult to accept compliments can agree that it is worse to have your efforts and undertakings completely ignored by those around you. Ignorance of these efforts and successes demotivates us. What is the point of working hard if no one actually celebrates it? As teachers, then, we need to praise our learners in meaningful, genuine and wholehearted ways. In order to truly embed praise within our classroom culture, we must also give learners opportunities to praise their peers. Finally, we can model the giving and, crucially, the receiving of compliments and praise to our learners. If a learner tells you that you are a good teacher, don't blush and disagree, muttering about your Year 10 group's mock exam results; accept their compliment in the way that you would want them to accept a compliment from you. A simple 'Thank you' and a smile will not make you appear arrogant or conceited. If you constantly find ways of negating or refuting positive feedback, then your learners will follow your lead and feel uncomfortable in accepting praise from outside and from others, preventing the development of a positive classroom culture.

CASE STUDY

In a Year 4 class in a primary school in the East Midlands, a recently qualified teacher – who had previous experience of working with children with behavioural difficulties in the social care setting – adopted a strategy of using meaningful, specific and regular praise in order to quickly establish a positive relationship with learners who had experienced behavioural difficulties previously within their time at the school. The teacher identified three learners who could potentially lose focus and engagement during the school day, which could lead to further disruptive behaviours, and sought out opportunities to praise them individually for carrying out classroom routines. The teacher did not always do this publicly, in front of the whole class, but made time to go over to each student and praise them, for instance when they had entered the classroom and quickly embarked upon the starter activity. By taking the time to identify learners who could become distracted and deliberately making the most of every opportunity to praise their positive behaviours, the teacher prevented any escalation of negative behaviours and ensured that the classroom environment remained positive, respectful and friendly to these learners who had previously experienced conflict within the classroom as a result of unwanted behaviour and subsequent teacher challenge. This proactive approach, rather than the reactive sanctioning of negative behaviours, enabled the learners to develop a love of learning and a positive view of school and education. All three learners developed in terms of their confidence, maturity and attitude, with no negative behaviour incidents taking place over the course of the year. For one of these students, this was a complete transformation, having been reprimanded on induction day by the head teacher for swearing in class.

Modelling positive behaviours

The importance of modelling behaviour is rooted in social learning theory, with Bandura outlining that: 'modelling influences produce learning principally through their informative functions ... rather than specific stimulus-response associations' (1971: 6). In this way, it is more likely that pupils will learn positive behaviours from modelling rather than through reward or sanctions of desirable or undesirable behaviours. Bandura highlights the four key steps involved in this type of modelling as relating to attention, retention, motoric reproduction and finally, reinforcement and motivation. With regard to attention, Bandura foregrounds the importance of learners paying attention to models because 'a person cannot learn much by observation if he does not attend to, or recognize, the essential features of the model's behaviour' (ibid.: 6). As such, teachers need to draw attention to the behaviours that they themselves are modelling as well as explicitly identify these desired behaviours when they are modelled by other learners. Learners must deliberately pay attention to these models in order for the modelling to be effective. Subsequently, in order for a learner to draw on these models when they are no longer present, they must be able to retain the memory of the behaviours. Memories can be coded visually or verbally, with the latter typifying 'most of the cognitive processes that regulate behavior' (ibid.: 7).

Bandura also highlights the potential of 'verbal coding of ... visual information' through 'symbolic coding' (ibid.) for improving longer-term retention of actions and behaviours. He states that 'observers who code modelled activities into either words, concise labels, or vivid imagery learn and retain the behaviour better than those who simply observe or are mentally preoccupied with other matters while watching the performance of others' (ibid.). For teachers, learners could be charged with coding behaviours as positive or negative within the learning environment, tracking these and perhaps deciding on their own labels, images or guides to positive behaviours as a way of initially establishing expectations within the classroom. Learners could create visual symbols of observed positive behaviours which they could then share with one another, ensuring that behaviour expectations are rooted in a collaborative and reciprocal process and are attended to and remembered by learners.

Next, learners need to be given the opportunity to reproduce modelled behaviours. Regardless of the quality of the model, if the learner is not given the freedom to attempt to mimic each step of the desired behaviour, it is unlikely they will retain the memory of it. Again, this emphasises the importance of agency and increasing independence within the learning environment. For example, a teacher who wishes to model high-quality speaking and listening within the classroom must give learners the opportunity to practise these skills with an increasing degree of independence, embracing the risk of learners finding this difficult or circumnavigating the task if they choose to.

Finally, Bandura outlines the importance of 'reinforcement and motivational processes' (ibid.: 8) in prompting learners to manifest positive behaviours. He explains that 'when positive incentives are provided, observational learning, which previously remained unexpressed, is promptly translated into action' (ibid.). In this way, teachers need to ensure that they incentivise positive behaviours through praise and other forms of reinforcement. This positive feedback also addresses the difficulties that sometimes arise during the phase where a learner attempts to reproduce behaviours, with their efficacy being somewhat limited in that they are often unable to witness their own behaviours and therefore can struggle to emulate accurately. Through praise of positive behaviours, the teacher and other learners can reinforce the learner's attempts at replicating behaviours and reassure them when these attempts are successful, guiding them further, as appropriate, if they struggle.

Modelling is a key principle of high-quality teaching and learning, with most practitioners understanding the importance of this technique when delivering curriculum content. By applying Bandura's social learning theory to behaviour, the same principles can clearly be used to encourage positive interactions within the classroom, sustaining a positive environment that is authentic and collaborative. As Bandura says, 'simply exposing persons to models does not in itself ensure that they will attend closely to them' (ibid.: 6). Teachers cannot just discretely embody the values of the classroom; they must explain, model, promote and praise positive learning behaviours, consistently across all areas of their practice.

CASE STUDY

An experienced English teacher wanted to further develop the positive atmosphere of her classroom by moving from a typical classroom feedback structure, where she alone praised learner behaviours, to a more empowered model, where learners felt comfortable with praising one another. The teacher explained to the students that they were going to complete a group work activity during the lesson, but that as well as focusing on the task itself, they needed to provide specific and meaningful feedback to the person sitting next to them, in the form of a compliment at the end of the activity. The learners completed their activity and then the teacher distributed mini whiteboards and pens so that they could write down their compliment. As the learners were writing their compliments down during the specified time, the teacher had the opportunity to circulate and ensure that all compliments were relevant and met the agreed criteria. The teacher then directed the feedback of the learners, who took it in turns to praise one another, with some insightful and heartfelt declarations of admiration being made. You could adapt this activity and the format of the feedback for different results. First, the feedback could take place in pairs, with learners being given 30 seconds each to share their compliment with their partner and then swap over, so that all learners are speaking simultaneously and the activity is fast-paced. Alternatively, in order to showcase the positive behaviours of the class during the activity and their strengths in providing positive praise to one another publicly, the teacher could structure the feedback so that students take it in turns to praise one another in groups or even as a whole class, perhaps with a round of applause at the end to celebrate these collective achievements.

General praise

We praise in order to make positive actions noteworthy, encouraging learners to link positive behaviours with a positive consequence, as illustrated in the discussion of the principles of modelling as part of Bandura's social learning theory. We also praise so as to increase the chance of all learners in a classroom paying attention to model behaviour. Less mechanistically than this, however, we praise because it feels like the right thing to do when we are met with high levels of effort, commitment or determination. Recent psychological research relating to positive psychology affords classroom teachers even more opportunities to use praise effectively within learning environments. Korthagen places 'the deficiency model in education' (2013:) within the context of wider psychological thought and subsequently asserts the potential of applying key features of the branch of positive psychology, which came to oppose the dominance of the deficiency model, within educational settings. Korthagen (ibid.), drawing on the work of Seligman and Csikszentmihalyi (2000), proposes an emphasis on '*character strengths* such as creativity, courage, perseverance, kindness and fairness' (Korthagen, 2013: 14, italics in original) for support and development of teachers. These core qualities, exemplified in more detail through the Values in Action (VIA) character virtues that we explored in Chapter 2, can also be identified and praised within learners, offering teachers the opportunity to praise positive actions in the context of a learner's own positive character traits. If we take one of the VIA character virtues as an example, such as curiosity, a teacher can praise any manifestation of this quality within learner behaviour. A statement such as 'I like that you ask lots of questions about the text because it shows your curiosity' creates positive links between the learner's behaviour and their character, resulting in a positive form of labelling. Exemplification of key character strengths in classroom behaviours could potentially help to foreground the importance of character strengths rather than deficiencies, rooting the learning environment in positivity rather than negativity. The specific nature of these character strengths and the behaviours that reflect them also allows teachers to focus on particular behaviours that merit praise, providing positive feedback that is specific and therefore helps to reinforce specific actions. By avoiding vague and general praise, which can be completely meaningless and therefore ineffective, the teacher is once again able to reinforce and motivate learners to imitate specific positive behaviours, using social learning theory in order to sustain an effective and positive classroom culture.

Subject-specific praise

When considering praise, it is also important to reflect on subject-specific praise, which, similarly to the observational learning through modelling that can be used to encourage positive learning behaviours, can be used in order to foreground the importance of particular qualities within the work that learners produce. It can be argued that the increased focus on written forms of assessment in the English education system, which resulted in the conclusion that 'marking – providing written feedback on pupils' work – has become disproportionately valued by schools and has become unnecessarily burdensome for teachers' (Department for Education (DfE), 2016), could be seen as conforming to the psychological deficiency model, with some teachers placing an emphasis on target-setting in order to meet expectations of high quantities of written feedback. The DfE's Marking Policy Review Group also concluded that overly detailed forms of written feedback 'can be dispiriting, for both teacher and pupil, by failing to encourage and engender motivation and resilience' (ibid.: 7). An increased positive emphasis on the academic aspects of core qualities within teacher marking could help to inspire learners and empower them to use their existing strengths in order to develop their own skills, rather than focusing on the deficiencies shown in their classwork. In this way, the social and academic expectations of learners can overlap through the common framework of core qualities or character strengths, casting the learning experience as a journey of personal development through which learners take increasing responsibility for themselves and their own learning.

CASE STUDY

A teacher of a Year 5 class was using written marking to assess learners' abilities to use adverbs at the start of sentences. One learner had either misunderstood or rejected the task and had used verbs at the start of sentences, instead. The teacher took the opportunity to praise the core quality of creativity that the learner had shown in approaching the task in a different way that still fulfilled the goal of varying their sentence structures, using this as the basis for a further challenge to experiment with adverbs, which were emphasised when the original task was set. The teacher used their written feedback to emphasise the idea that using many different sentence types could allow the learner to exercise their creativity even more effectively by providing them with more choices when they construct sentences. Here, the learner was not reprimanded for approaching the task in a way that, according to the deficiency model, would be seen as wrong, but rather, their core qualities were identified, praised and redirected in order for them to fulfil the demands of the task as part of their own learning journey.

Managing negative behaviours

It is important to recognise the subjective nature of behaviour within the classroom. As with any group situation, teachers and learners may interpret different behaviours in different ways, potentially leading to miscommunication and misunderstanding. In light of this, it is important to empathise with others and to consider the potential reasons behind their actions. Teachers should avoid taking learners' behaviour personally, acknowledging that learners often behave in particular ways in an attempt to elicit particular responses from their peers or because they have not considered the consequences of their actions. As a teacher, it is important to identify what behaviours you see as negative. For example, some teachers insist on silence during particular activities, whereas others prefer a more flexible working environment. You need to have a good idea of what behaviours you do want to encourage and what behaviours you want to discourage in order to consistently promote positive actions within the classroom.

Suggestions and tips for dealing with a lack of cooperation

- *Keep it simple*: What are the overarching principles that learners need to adopt in order for a purposeful, harmonious environment to be established? Rather than listing multiple rules that learners should follow, simplifying your expectations into one or two crucial expectations that are clearly explained in the context of the classroom's values makes these easier to follow. A rule such as 'Do not speak over the teacher or your classmates when they are speaking' is grounded in mutual respect and the need to listen carefully to one another.

- *Make it easy to follow*: Teachers can also clearly signpost the specific ways in which positive behaviour can be shown, operationalising the concept. For example, in a class that is particularly talkative and not necessarily engaged with the task set by the teacher, the teacher can identify explicit behaviours that they are looking for, explaining how these will show the students' success in meeting expectations. If a learner is giving feedback to the whole class, then the teacher could tell the class that she wants to see everyone looking at the learner who is speaking so that it is clear that they are listening. Such instructions can sometimes feel a little awkward initially, but by approaching this with a degree of lightheartedness and humour, the teacher can release the pressure learners feel when speaking to a wider audience and make it easy for learners to cooperate by clearly identifying the desired behaviours practically. The specific nature of the phrase 'I want to see you do . . .', rather than 'Listen carefully', makes it far easier for learners to showcase positive behaviours successfully.
- *Keep the focus on the behaviour*: When sanctioning negative behaviours, it is important that the *behaviour* is explicitly identified as the issue rather than the learner themselves. 'You're rude' is far more inflammatory and damaging than a simple statement of fact such as: 'Talking over people is rude.'

Despite valuing the agency of all of the learners in your classroom, creating an environment rooted in care and compassion, and consistently applying your behaviour philosophy to every situation, there are still going to be times when learners refuse to cooperate. They are human, after all.

Beyond this, it is important that you remain calm and committed to your principles. Where you have identified and sanctioned negative behaviours, it is helpful to quickly find opportunities to genuinely praise cooperative behaviour in order to re-establish the positive tone of the classroom environment. This also ensures that a learner who has been sanctioned does not see this as a personal attack, but understands that you are simply acting objectively in your comments on behaviour. Usually, the learner quickly realises that you are paying close attention to their behaviour and prefers meaningful praise to other reminders of classroom expectations. It is important that this praise is genuine and not patronising. 'Well done for presenting your work so neatly, this will really help with revision later' is far more effective than a simple 'Well done', which is not rooted in a specific learning behaviour.

For a learner who clearly struggles with concentration or cooperation over the course of a whole lesson, it is important to gain knowledge of their behaviour baseline and then gradually increase the expectation of their positive behaviours in order to deepen their understanding of social expectations. With these sometimes high-profile learners, who struggle to cooperate in many lessons and show a high degree of discomfort within the school system overall, tactical ignoring can be useful. As a teacher, you need to carefully balance the impression that you have an all-seeing eye, which the learners cannot evade, with the role you need to take in order to deliver your lesson effectively. In order to fulfil these sometimes competing roles, it may be necessary to tactically ignore some learner behaviours in order to avoid disrupting the learning of an entire class.

CASE STUDY

In a lesson observed by their mentor, a trainee teacher was teaching a mixed ability Year 11 group about the format of their examinations for GCSE English Language. The teacher had been struggling with maintaining control of verbal contributions previously as they had been accepting responses from students who were shouting out over their peers rather than volunteering to share their ideas by raising their hands or waiting their turn to be asked by the teacher. After a discussion with their mentor regarding the possible reasons behind this behaviour, the teacher decided to use tactical ignoring in order to encourage these evidently keen learners to share their ideas in a way that did not dominate the group. The teacher asked the group an open question and ignored the responses that were shouted out, asking a student who had raised their hand to share their response. The teacher then praised the learner for their answer and also their behaviour, with the comment 'Well done for raising your hand to share your ideas. It's so important for us all to take turns and have the chance to speak'. In this way, the teacher successfully signposted positive behaviour without having to waste lesson time challenging individual learners over their lack of compliance. With regular reinforcement of this strategy throughout the lesson and in subsequent lessons, the learners who had been shouting out their ideas and dominating the lessons made a conscious effort to fulfil the teacher's expectations of their behaviour. This led to a more productive and positive atmosphere within the classroom as all learners had the opportunity to share their views, which were valued equally by their peers and their teacher.

It can also be useful to identify negative behaviours without speaking so as to avoid disrupting the flow of a sequence of activities. Through eye contact, body language and gestures, teachers can reinforce behaviour expectations discreetly. When learners are completing an independent written task, for example, the teacher can avoid publicly challenging a learner who appears to be daydreaming and has not yet picked up their pen, by miming the action of writing or gesturing for them to speed up. With a toolkit of natural, regularly used gestures, a teacher can silently reinforce expectations.

If a learner's behaviour is causing severe disruption

The benefit of talking without a wider audience cannot be overestimated when dealing with disruptive behaviour. It is important to always value the learner's view and opinion, and this type of conversation usually needs to take place away from the learner's peer group so that their thoughts and words are not influenced by the persona that they are trying to show to their peers. It can be useful when beginning a difficult conversation to root the discussion in your concern for the learner's well-being. Ask them how they are. A learner may be behaving in an unusual way for a particular reason, and it is important for you to show that you still value them as a person despite having had to sanction them. It can be surprising how effective a firm but fair conversation can be with a learner who has behaved disruptively, particularly when skills such as empathy are developed through questioning. 'Why have I asked you to step outside?', 'Why did you do that?', 'Was that a good thing to do?' and 'Did that help you to make progress in your learning today?' are all valuable questions when you are trying to unpick the reasons behind and consequences of a learner's behaviour. Sometimes, an attitude of professed incomprehension combined with fact-finding questions can be particularly effective. It is far more impactful to be allowed to admit your own mistakes and the negative effects that they may have had than to be simply reprimanded for disobedience by an overbearing and potentially aggressive teacher.

Growing a school culture

Establishing a positive classroom ethos and striving to uphold this as a key principle of the educational experience is a significant achievement and is worth celebrating. To develop the potential of the classroom environment further, however, it is important to embed this positive and collaborative belief system in every classroom within a school. Gregory and Ripski (2008) highlight the importance of trust within relationships between all participants within educational institutions, and cite the work of Bryk and Schneider (2002), which found that 'elementary schools with higher relational trust were more likely to achieve successful organizational reform as measured through gains in math and reading achievement' (Gregory and Ripski, 2008: 340). Here, the significance of trust within not just the teacher–learner relationship but also the educational institution's values as a whole, is foregrounded and is seen as a precursor to success. It is also important to recognise that the schools that were identified as featuring high levels of relational trust succeeded in concrete, measurable ways. A positive, empowering culture is not an idealistic utopian dream with only qualitative impact, but a valid, effective means of engaging, motivating and empowering learners to achieve within the education system.

The evidence that positivity and trust within schools has a positive impact on learner outcomes is compelling, but it is crucial to remember that a school cannot commit to an ethos on a superficial level. Simply composing a new school mission statement and displaying some inspiring posters is not the same as embedding and sustaining a positive school culture. Interestingly, and perhaps frustratingly, if a school only strives to become a positive place in the vague hope that learner attainment will subsequently improve, then their efforts are unlikely to succeed. A successful model for a positive learning culture needs to focus on the principles and values of the students, staff and then, considering all of these, the school as the overarching community that represents these values in a shared, unified form. Again, these principles and values cannot be solely identified by a survey or questionnaire, but instead both students and staff need to be given the opportunity to reflect on their beliefs and actions, identifying their own values and the ways in which they are reflected in their daily lives. As such, the school needs to value these beliefs, regardless of whether or not they are contradictory or unpopular, as only through genuinely listening to and valuing others can a truly positive culture be established. This wholehearted listening and acceptance of others' beliefs can be linked to Carl Rogers and his conviction that unconditional positive regard is a cornerstone of the relationship between student and teacher (Rogers et al., 2014). Likewise, this must be a cornerstone of the relationships between staff. A colleague may disagree with your views, beliefs or values, but, rather than viewing this from a binary perspective and seeing their agreement as a sign of total support and their disagreement as indicative of complete opposition, we must listen to and acknowledge their thoughts without allowing them to impact upon our view of them as a classroom practitioner or, indeed, our own self-image. Our students may not love the same books that we do, but we would not deliberately cultivate a negative relationship with them as a result of this. In the same way, school communities benefit from valuing differences in order to draw on and strengthen the significance of those values that are shared. Mr Lewis from the Maths Department may dislike your new classroom display, but that doesn't mean he thinks you're a bad teacher. It is also likely that his reasons for disliking your display are rooted in his own personal beliefs surrounding teaching and that he has come to this conclusion because he, like you, fervently believes in the importance of education for young people. Whether or not it is rude of him to make this known is another story.

Aggressive or assertive?

It can be tempting early on in your teaching career (and at various points later on) to try to adopt the teaching strategies of successful colleagues in a bid to become an equally successful practitioner yourself. Where behaviour is concerned, as well as other aspects of teaching and learning, it is important to remember that teachers cannot become other people with different personalities and attitudes. Teachers, and their schools, must remember that they are human beings: individuals who should embrace differences rather than slavishly strive for conformity at the expense of confident creativity. There seems to be a fallacy that a 'one-size-fits-all' approach can solve all the challenges faced by the education system. In the same way, a teacher needs to find their own style for promoting positive learning behaviours, which fits with both their personal philosophy and the core qualities of their personality.

In a study based in Israel, China and Australia, Romi et al. identified four teacher behaviours as aggressive and therefore resulting in 'distraction negativity [by learners] toward teachers and [learners'] perceptions that teachers' responses were un-justified' (2011: 231). The behaviours that Romi et al. identified as aggressive were as follows:

- Yells angrily at students who misbehave.
- Deliberately embarrasses students who misbehave.
- Keeps the class in because some students misbehave.
- Makes sarcastic comments to students who misbehave. (Ibid.: 236)

At first glance, this criticism of sarcasm and collective punishment could condemn as aggressive some of the best teachers we have ever known. Herein lies the great difficulty at the heart of promoting positive behaviour. The relationship between teacher and learner is bilateral and the terms of that relationship are negotiated by both parties. If a teacher's sarcastic sense of humour delights the class and empowers them to uphold the positive behaviours of their learning environment, then how can this be seen as aggressive? Humour is a particularly effective tool in defusing conflict and difficult situations and therefore the context of teacher behaviours must be taken into consideration before they are branded 'aggressive' in their approach. Romi et al. (2011: 237) found that the 'relative impact of sarcasm on students' negativity was low' in Israel, perhaps indicating that this teacher's behaviour is not always aggressive or confrontational, emphasising the importance of the cultural context of social behaviours.

Similarly, Romi et al. acknowledge that: 'in a truly collective community . . . [collective] punishment may be argued to be more justifiable, particularly if all group members were empowered to encourage each other to act responsibly' (2011: 238). Again, this highlights a difficulty with branding certain teacher behaviours as aggressive, with the context of these behaviours being crucial to understanding the intentions of the teacher and the subsequent perceptions of the learner of these behaviours.

The identification of certain behaviours as characteristic of certain teaching styles also poses a problem, in that it is generally considered important for teachers to be assertive within the classroom so that they are able to praise and sanction learner behaviours with authority. The line between aggressiveness and assertiveness can be blurred and it would be damaging to assert that teachers should reject certain behaviours that are actually positive and effective for them through fear of these being misconstrued by third-party observers.

With regard to the impact of the wider learning community on the classroom environment, schools should provide a framework for teachers to draw on for support in dealing with behaviour; however, it is unlikely to be effective if they heavily prescribe the details of classroom logistics, thereby denigrating the professional judgement, know-how and intuition of the classroom practitioner. A teacher is a human being; a learner is a human being. We must realise that the interactions between the two are unique, personal and incredibly important.

Chapter summary

- The relationship between learners and teachers is particularly effective when both parties are united in their shared goal of educational and personal development.
- The relationship between teacher and learner is not unilateral but bilateral and reciprocal, with each interaction shaping and developing the values and identity of all the participants.

- Positive relationships can be achieved by:
  - establishing positive interactions with learners by getting to know their interests
  - using meaningful and genuine praise in order to highlight positive classroom behaviours
  - modelling positive behaviours and giving learners the opportunity to reproduce these behaviours with an increasing degree of independence.
- Teachers should avoid taking learners' behaviour personally and instead see it as the result of a variety of different factors.
- Teachers can manage negative behaviours by:
  - considering what behaviours they want to encourage and what behaviours they want to discourage
  - ensuring that the principles of the classroom values are simple and easy to understand, with behaviour expectations rooted in this philosophy
  - ensuring that verbal sanctions are focused on the undesired action rather than on the learner themselves
  - using tactical ignoring when necessary
  - using non-verbal actions to identify negative behaviours without speaking, helping to minimise the impact of an audience on individuals' behaviours
  - using empathetic questioning in order to encourage a learner to reflect on their disruptive behaviour.
- A school culture rooted in trust is important in encouraging positive behaviour in every classroom.
- Different teachers will have different styles and ways of dealing with particular behaviours: it is important to value differences and examine these in context.

Further reading

Korthagen, F.A.J., Kim, Y.M. and Greene, W.L. (eds) (2013) *Teaching and Learning from Within: A Core Reflection Approach to Quality and Inspiration in Education*. New York: Routledge.
If you are interested in how core strengths can be used to underpin professional development in order to deal with challenges such as managing behaviour, then you may enjoy this book.

Saito, E. et al. (2015) 'School reform for positive behaviour support through collaborative learning: Utilising lesson study for a learning community', *Cambridge Journal of Education*, 45 (4): 489–518.
If you would like an example of how a positive behaviour culture can influence learner behaviour then see this article.

Bibliography

Bandura, A. (1971) *Social Learning Theory*. New York: General Learning Press.
Bryk, A.S. and Schneider, B. (2002) *Trust in Schools: A Core Resource for Improvement*. New York: Russell Sage Foundation.
Cornelius-White, J. (2007) 'Learner-centered teacher–student relationships are effective: A meta-analysis', *Review of Educational Research*, 77 (1): 113–43.
Department for Education (DfE) (2016) 'Eliminating unnecessary workload around marking'. Available at: http://www.gov.uk/government/publications/reducing-teacher-workload-marking-policy-review-group-report (accessed 10 August 2016).
Gregory, A. and Ripski, M.B. (2008) 'Adolescent trust in teachers: Implications for behavior in the high school classroom', *School Psychology Review*, 37 (3): 337–53.
Korthagen, F.A.J. (2013) 'The core reflection approach', in F.A.J. Korthagen, Y.M. Kim and W.L. Greene (eds), *Teaching and Learning from Within: A Core Reflection Approach to Quality and Inspiration in Education*. New York: Routledge.
Kuczynski, L. (2003) 'Beyond bidirectionality: Bilateral conceptual frameworks for understanding dynamics in parent–child relations', in L. Kuczynski (ed.), *Handbook of Dynamics in Parent–Child Relations*. London: Sage.
Nurmi, J.-E. (2012) 'Students' characteristics and teacher–child relationships in instruction: A meta-analysis', *Educational Research Review*, 7 (3): 177–97.
Rogers, C.R., Lyon, H.C. and Tausch, R. (2014) *On Becoming an Effective Teacher*. London: Routledge.
Romi, S., Lewis, R., Roache, J. and Riley, P. (2011) 'The impact of teachers' aggressive management techniques on students' attitudes to schoolwork', *Journal of Educational Research*, 104 (4): 231–40.
Seligman, M.E. and Csikszentmihalyi, M. (2000) 'Positive psychology: An introduction', *American Psychologist*, 55 (1): 5–14.

5

WELL-BEING AND SAFEGUARDING PUPILS AND TEACHERS

Chapter guide

In this chapter, you will learn about:

- Current concerns of pupils and teachers
- Complex aspects of well-being and safeguarding of pupils and teachers
- Risk factors: Accountability without responsibility, isolation, basic needs, cultural needs
- Protective factors: Validation, social and peer support, flourishing and existing
- Approaches to well-being in pupils and teachers
- Understanding the roles teachers and other professionals play in relation to safeguarding

There is plenty of evidence to suggest that some pupils and teachers have been having a tough time in schools in recent years. Concerns are particularly focused on safeguarding, mental health and well-being of children and their teachers. On the one hand, there is evidence that more and younger children are experiencing mental health difficulties. Research on teacher supply suggests that about 30 per cent of teachers leave the profession after five years (Foster, 2018: 1). There are many complex reasons for this, but one of them suggests that workload and teacher stress are for some teachers too much. On the other hand, many staff do cope and thoroughly enjoy working with children and young people. Rather than draining teachers, many children energise and inspire teachers. We therefore argue that well-being is a complex concept, varying for pupils and teachers and also at different stages in life. Links between well-being and safeguarding are made explicit: caring for pupils and early career teachers is seen as being central to achieving effective education in schools.

As with intrinsic motivation, we argue that the quality of relationships (connectedness), personal and professional control (autonomy) and, ultimately, personal growth (self-actualisation) are at the heart of well-being for both young people and their teachers. Whilst there has been a growing focus on mental health and well-being in young people, we believe that there has been less emphasis and value placed on the mental health and well-being of teachers. Issues of neglect, and in particular of psychological neglect, are discussed in relation to mental health and resilience for both pupils and teachers. The two are most definitely connected. How can we expect to develop the well-being of pupils if we don't pay equal attention to that of their teachers? For both young people and teachers, we explore protective and risk factors. What leads to a culture of well-being in schools? Communication, relationships and voice are all explored as elements of a successful and healthy school.

Current concerns of pupils and teachers

In 2015, the Safeguarding Boards Business Office sent out Safeguarding Surveys to primary and secondary school students in one part of England (Leicestershire and Rutland Safeguarding Children Board, 2015). The results show that many pupils are concerned about their well-being and have a number of worries:

- Over 46 per cent of primary school children are worried about nobody listening to them.
- Over 43 per cent of primary school children are worried about their future.
- Over 62 per cent of secondary school students are worried about feeling stressed and not coping.
- Over 51 per cent of secondary school students are worried about being approached by a stranger when out.

The survey suggests some consistent themes in the students' answers around bullying, their online behaviours, the family, the school and, more generally, around coping and well-being.

REFLECTION POINT

In the following list of worries in primary and secondary students, think about to what extent these concerns reflect those of the students you teach.

Bullying

- Being bullied at school and online

Online

- Being approached by a stranger online
- Spending too much time online
- Being left out from online groups

Family

- Family worries
- Family quarrels
- Health worries about my family
- Family money worries
- Parents telling me off

School

- Not doing well at school
- Being told off at school

Coping and well-being

- Nobody listening to me
- Feeling stressed, can't cope
- Worries about my own health
- Being hurt by people
- Drink and drugs: People doing drugs and drinking too much
- Being approached by a stranger when out
- My future

Of course, pupils are still young and in their formative years, but they only lack the experiences that are eventually reflected in the adult concerns and worries later in life. Every teacher who emerges from teacher training was at one time one of these children. Worries, coping and well-being are clearly ongoing issues in life.

On the one side, pupils are concerned for themselves and their families. From the teacher's perspective, they are not only concerned with trying to deal with these worries and concerns in a way that promotes growth and a good education for children and young people, they also have their own concerns about their jobs, families and the way their school is developing. Sometimes, this can be against a backdrop of heightened pressure and a spotlight on the work of teachers. Teachers are therefore dealing with their own pressures as well as the challenges of their pupils, often in a pressure-cooker atmosphere of accountability. No wonder many teachers leave the profession only a few years into their early careers. In the National Foundation for Educational Research (NFER) report *Engaging Teachers: NFER Analysis of Teacher Retention* (Lynch, 2016), workload was a key factor in around 10 per cent of teachers leaving in their first year of teaching and in 30 per cent of those leaving within five years of qualifying. Inspection and policy change were key drivers for increased workload, which then led to poor health and feeling undervalued.

Much recent discussion of teacher well-being has focused on the issue of workload in school (National Union of Teachers (NUT), 2014). According to the NUT, evidence of staff workloads in England suggests that primary teachers work an average of 60 hours in a week and secondary teachers around 63 hours. Working regulations suggest that head teachers are required to ensure that teachers experience a reasonable work–life balance. The head teacher has a duty to 'lead and manage staff with a proper regard for their well-being and legitimate expectations, including the expectation of a healthy balance between work and other commitments' (NUT, 2014: 35). Of course, workload is an important aspect of the health and safety of teachers in their workplace, but it is not the only concern that teachers have. Newly qualified teachers when completing a survey were asked why they might consider leaving the profession. Workload was high on the agenda, but so was perceived low respect for teachers in the media, perceived levels of change in schools (the curriculum, and terms and conditions for teachers), pupil behaviour in school, and the focus on performance and accountability through inspection by the regulatory body, Office for Standards in Education (Ofsted). Of course, there are many reasons why teachers came into the profession, such as the desire to inspire learners and the love of their subject.

Roberts-Holmes and Bradbury explain that current approaches to education in the early years in England are having a detrimental effect on both children and teachers. They describe the 'datification of early years' education' (2016: 600). They explain that increasing accountability associated with quantitative information on early years' outcomes suggests that children have become 'reconfigured as miniature centres of calculation' (ibid.: 600).

They go on to say that 'young children can be reduced to the school's statistical raw materials that are mined for their maximum productivity gains' (ibid.: 600). One teacher in their study said that her major concern was the well-being of her children, but that the development of meaningful relationships had been subjugated to the production of performance data (ibid.: 600). Robert-Holmes and Bradbury (ibid.) argue that this has an overall negative impact on both children and staff.

We need a language of well-being that recognises the needs of children as well as staff. Only by meeting the needs of pupils and teachers to the best of our ability will we be able to ensure that a school is both academically and professionally successful at a human level. In law, employers have a duty of care to their employees, which means that they should take all steps that are reasonably possible to ensure their health, safety and well-being (Donaldson Feilder and Podro, 2012). Demonstrating concern for the physical and mental health of your workers shouldn't just be seen as a legal duty – there's a clear business case, too. It can be a key factor in building trust and reinforcing your commitment to your employees, and can help improve staff retention, boost productivity and pave the way for greater employee engagement.

Legally, employers must abide by relevant health and safety and employment law, as well as the common law duty of care. They also have a moral and ethical duty not to cause, or fail to prevent, physical or psychological injury, and must fulfil their responsibilities with regard to personal injury and negligence claims.

Requirements under an employer's duty of care are wide-ranging and may manifest themselves in many different ways, such as:

- Clearly defining jobs and undertaking risk assessments
- Ensuring a safe work environment
- Providing adequate training and feedback on performance
- Ensuring that staff do not work excessive hours
- Providing areas for rest and relaxation
- Protecting staff from bullying or harassment, either from colleagues or third parties
- Protecting staff from discrimination
- Providing communication channels for employees to raise concerns
- Consulting employees on issues that concern them.

An employer can be deemed to have breached their duty of care by failing to do everything that was reasonable in the circumstances to keep the employee safe from harm. Employees also have responsibilities for their health and well-being at work – for example, they are entitled by law to refuse to undertake work that isn't safe without fear of disciplinary action.

Likewise, teachers have a duty of care towards their pupils under common law and statute. This used to be recognised in the term *in loco parentis*: a teacher was expected to act in the best interests of a child. This evolved and was formally recognised as part of a teachers' professionalism by the courts in 1962. The 'standard of care' expected of a teacher was held to be that of a person exhibiting the responsible mental qualities of a prudent parent in the circumstances of school, rather than home life. The current standard of care expected of a teacher is that of a reasonable person in the circumstances of a class teacher (NUT, 2014). 'A duty of care' can be seen just as a legal requirement or moreover as a moral imperative to ensure that the school does everything to promote the cognitive, physical, social, emotional and moral well-being of the child. Wiley and Cory (2013) identify a long philosophical tradition that sees education as a focus on the whole child. For instance, the focus of Pestalozzi, the founder of elementary schools in Germany, was on a hands-on learning experience through objects and books that balances hands, heart and head. Others in the counselling tradition have seen spiritual factors as equally important in pupil well-being (Briggs et al., 2011). Briggs et al. (ibid.) argue that counsellors should recognise the spiritual dimension of the whole child. First, teachers might develop counselling skills, but they are not in most cases trained counsellors, carrying out a programme of treatment for the child. However, we do recognise, as World Faiths does, that the spiritual dimension to a child's life is equally important. Arguably, this dimension grows as a child grows and they start to exercise a desire for greater autonomy, meaning and purpose in their lives. However, in the UK, a rich moral and spiritual climate is widely recognised as a prerequisite for the education of the whole child, even from an early age.

Banyard et al. (2017) highlight risk and protective factors in a sample of American children. These are shown below:

> **Risk factors:** Poverty, a network of health services lack of family ties, stress and isolation are seen as risk factors in child maltreatment cases, as is living in an urban environment. But these elements can differ between cultures. For example, some religious communities can provide a network of support for the child at risk of maltreatment. Of course, there are well-documented cases of the Church being systematically involved in child abuse (Knaus, 2017).

> **Protective factors:** On the other hand, Banyard et al. (2017) suggest that good family and care networks, opportunities for developing meaning making and a voice in their learning all provide ways of coping and achieving high-quality outcomes in and out of school.

Of course, children can be vulnerable both in and out of school and there are particular responsibilities around the safeguard of children. Whilst this book cannot replace more detailed, country-specific and up-to-date advice on safeguarding, it is worth reiterating advice from the UK Department for Education (DfE):

1. Schools and colleges and their staff are an important part of the wider safeguarding system for children.
2. Safeguarding and promoting the welfare of children is **everyone's** responsibility. **Everyone** who comes into contact with children and their families and carers has a role to play in safeguarding children. In order to fulfil this responsibility effectively, all professionals should make sure their approach is child-centred. This means that they should consider, at all times, what is in the **best interests** of the child.
3. No single professional can have a full picture of a child's needs and circumstances. If children and families are to receive the right help at the right time, **everyone** who comes into contact with them has a role to play in identifying concerns, sharing information and taking prompt action.
4. Safeguarding and promoting the welfare of children is defined for these purposes as: protecting children from maltreatment; preventing impairment of children's health or development; ensuring that children grow up in circumstances consistent with the provision of safe and effective care; and taking action to enable all children to have the best outcomes.
5. Children includes everyone under the age of 18. (DfE, 2016: 5)

All school and college staff should be aware that abuse, neglect and safeguarding issues are rarely stand-alone events that can be covered by one definition or label. In most cases, multiple issues will overlap with one another:

Abuse: A form of maltreatment of a child. Somebody may abuse or neglect a child by inflicting harm or by failing to act to prevent harm. Children may be abused in a family or in an institutional or community setting by those known to them or, more rarely, by others (e.g., via the Internet). They may be abused by an adult or adults or by another child or children.

  Physical abuse: A form of abuse that may involve hitting, shaking, throwing, poisoning, burning or scalding, drowning, suffocating or otherwise causing physical harm to a child. Physical harm may also be caused when a parent or carer fabricates the symptoms of, or deliberately induces, illness in a child.

Emotional abuse: The persistent emotional maltreatment of a child such as to cause severe and adverse effects on the child's emotional development. It may involve, conveying to a child that they are worthless or unloved, inadequate, or valued only insofar as they meet the needs of another person. Some level of emotional abuse is involved in all types of maltreatment of a child, although it may occur alone.

Sexual abuse: Involves forcing or luring a child or young person to take part in sexual activities, not necessarily involving a high level of violence, whether or not the child is aware of what is happening. The activities may involve physical contact, including, for example, rape or oral sex or non-penetrative acts such as masturbation, kissing, rubbing and touching outside of clothing. They may also include non-contact activities, such as involving children in looking at, or in the production of, sexual images, watching sexual activities, encouraging children to behave in sexually inappropriate ways or grooming a child in preparation for abuse (including via the Internet). Sexual abuse is not solely perpetrated by adult males. Women can also commit acts of sexual abuse, as can other children.

Neglect: The persistent failure to meet a child's basic physical and/or psychological needs, likely to result in the serious impairment of the child's health or development. Neglect may occur during pregnancy as a result of maternal substance abuse. Once a child is born, neglect may involve a parent or carer failing to: provide adequate food, clothing and shelter (including exclusion from home or abandonment); protect a child from physical and emotional harm or danger; ensure adequate supervision (including the use of inadequate care-givers); or ensure access to appropriate medical care or treatment. It may also include neglect of, or unresponsiveness to, a child's basic emotional needs. (DfE, 2016)

This same advice lists requirements under safeguarding to protect children and young people from radicalisation. This comes after acts of terrorism in several countries in Europe and North America. Whilst some of these atrocities were carried out by terrorists from abroad, some were committed by extreme right-wing or Islamist perpetrators in the country in which they were born. Interestingly, a common theme in the radicalisation of young people as well as the sexual abuse of young people is 'grooming'. We highlight the concept of 'grooming' since this is an act of control by another person over a child or young person. Of course, the purposes are entirely different in sexual grooming and radicalisation, but it is worth recognising some commonalities:

Building a relationship: Often by developing an emotional connection. In 'sexual grooming', this may involve exploiting children through emotional control by a family friend. In radicalisation, this might involve exploiting dissatisfaction in young people through emotional manipulation, for instance on the Internet.

Building control: Through blackmail and by establishing a hold over a child. 'Revenge porn' is held as a threat by some in this situation. In radicalisation, greater and greater isolation from the normal family and peer group is used to insulate the radicalised young person. In some cases, this involves radicalisation on the Internet or even physically in training camps outside of the country.

Building secrecy: Through blackmail or telling a child they will be in trouble if they tell anyone. Likewise, secrecy is a precursor in some cases to actual terrorist acts through manipulation by external extremists.

If a child is 'groomed' for sexual purposes, then this is a criminal act and an abuse of the child. UK government advice suggests that radicalisation follows a similar pattern and should be considered as a safeguarding issue in schools and colleges:

Many teenagers look for answers to questions about identity, faith and belonging, and are in search of adventure and excitement. Extremist groups claim to offer answers, and provide a strong sense of identity to vulnerable young people. Though instances are rare, even young children may be exposed to extremism, both inside and outside the home, or online.

Extremist groups are sophisticated in their use of the Internet and social media and this is often how they spread their ideology. This has made young people more susceptible to extremism, whether from Islamists or the far right.

You already help safeguard pupils from drugs, gangs and sexual exploitation. Radicalisation can have a similarly devastating effect on individuals, families and communities. Protecting pupils from the influence of extremist ideas is an important part of your overall safeguarding role. (DfE, 2017)

It is important that all professionals and pupils recognise the importance of safeguarding in schools and colleges. Of course, children and young people can be particularly vulnerable by virtue of their age and stage of development. However, protecting them is about making them strong with knowledge, control and a powerful voice. Thus, we believe that empowering children and young people, a central tenet of this book, is an important protective factor in safeguarding. Recent serious case reviews in child abuse cases state that different agencies (schools, social services and health services) do not always listen effectively to children. Communication always involves having something to say, having a way to say it, and importantly the will to say it. Schools, therefore, should include in their curriculum the knowledge and language children need in order to guard their own safety. Safeguarding should never just be seen as a responsibility of the child, but we must value children and promote their ability to protect themselves. For instance, whilst filters and monitoring systems can protect children to a certain extent on the Internet, it is even more important that they have the knowledge and motivation to protect themselves, as well as the will to share with adults any concerns; and, where they are unsure, that they can speak to a trusted and responsible adult who values their views. Whilst it is important that suitable and appropriate professionals are recruited to teach children, there needs to be an equivalent effort in schools to monitor the effectiveness of steps to value and empower children to make healthy decisions in their interests which protect both their short-term and long-term well-being. Some people would argue that there has been too much emphasis on creating a bureaucracy of safeguarding children in England, through various checking systems for professionals, which is not balanced with a sufficient value of the individual child. The danger is that schools can become places of compliance both for teachers and children. We argue here for a development in school safeguarding to engage, motivate and empower children and young people to have a strong voice, with appropriate knowledge. Knowledge, control and engagement in safeguarding empowers children and young people (Khan, 2016).

Save the Children (2010) identify the role of participation as being essential in their work. A number of charity workers have themselves been accused of abuse, so safeguarding children and vulnerable young people is even more important. This is not exclusively about safeguarding children, but it does provide a framework through which we would involve children in a school curriculum that safeguards children through empowerment:

Assigned but informed: Adults decide on the safeguarding curriculum and children are protected through it. The children understand the curriculum and they know how the curriculum helps to protect them. Adults respect children's views.

Adult-initiated, shared decisions with children: Adults have the initial idea of the safeguarding curriculum but children are involved in every step of the planning and implementation. Children's views are considered, and they are involved in making decisions.

Consulted and informed: The curriculum for safeguarding is designed and run by adults but children are consulted. They have a full understanding of the processes and their opinions are taken seriously.

Child-initiated and directed: Opportunities are created in school which enable children to direct a curriculum for safeguarding. This recognises the rights of children. Children have the initial idea and decide on how to exercise their rights. Adults are available but don't take charge.

Child-initiated, shared decisions with adults: Children have ideas, set up projects to exercise their rights in school and come to adults for advice, discussion and support. The adults don't direct but offer their expertise for young people to consider. (Adapted from Treseder and Smith (1997)).

REFLECTION POINT

Consider your own professional context:

- How much of the curriculum that you have created proactively helps children to be empowered in safeguarding their needs?
- What opportunities are there for teachers to really listen to children and respect their rights in school?
- Have schools got the balance right between the bureaucracy and accountability of safeguarding and creating a climate of empowering children that develops resilient young people who have a strong voice and are able to speak up for themselves when there is a problem?

In this reflection, we introduce the concept of children's rights in safeguarding. Children have a right to be safe, healthy and well, and to be able to speak up and to be listened to and acted upon if things are not right.

Approaches to well-being in pupils and teachers

Safeguarding can be seen as a process of policing a set of external rules and regulating the satisfaction of children's needs. On the other hand, it can be seen as set of rights to empower children, and, indeed, their teachers. For this reason, we focus on the concepts of children's rights. Human rights are rights inherent to all human beings, whatever our nationality, place of residence, sex, national or ethnic origin, colour, religion, language or any other status. We are all equally entitled to our human rights, without discrimination. These rights are all interrelated, interdependent and indivisible (United Nations, 1948; Detrick, 1999).

Universal human rights are often expressed and guaranteed by law in the forms of treaties, customary international law, general principles and other sources of international law. International human rights law lays down the obligations of governments to act in certain ways or to refrain from certain acts in order to promote and protect human rights and fundamental freedoms of individuals or groups.

Centuries ago, children's rights were rarely seen as important as they were seen to be the responsibility of the parents and children were not considered to have rights of their own. Jean-Jacques Rousseau changed much of the thinking about what it means to be a child with his book *Emile, or On Education* (1991 [1762]), which focused on a perceived period of innocence in childhood before the onset of adult life. From Rousseau onwards, the role of childhood and the protection of children has become a focus in children's rights. Several reformers such as the English jurist William Blackstone and Thomas Spence began to describe a set of rights for children from the later 1700s in England. In parallel with the wider commitment to human rights, the League of Nations adopted the Geneva Declaration of the Rights of the Child in 1924 [2009], which articulated the following children's rights:

- The right to receive the requirements for normal development,
- the right of the hungry child to be fed,
- the right of the sick child to receive health care,
- the right of the backward child to be reclaimed,
- the right of orphans to shelter, and
- the right to protection from exploitation.

The Declaration of the Rights of the Child is an international document promoting children's rights, and was drafted by Eglantyne Jebb and adopted by the League of Nations in 1924. It was adopted in an extended form by the United Nations in 1959 and implemented as the UN Convention on the Rights of Children in UK law in 1992. It is such an important document, that we reproduce 16 articles of the declaration in summary in Table 5.1. The full text can be found on the United Nations Children's Fund (UNICEF) website (2017).

Everything that is important in safeguarding and the empowerment of children is captured in this statement of the rights of children. The Convention must be understood as a whole: all rights are linked and no right is more important than another. The right to relax and play (Article 31) and the right to freedom of expression (Article 13) are as important as the right to be safe from violence (Article 19) and the right to education (Article 28). A number of schools around the world, including many in the UK, have recognised the UN rights of children in their schools. This takes safeguarding beyond bureaucratic policing to consider the whole child in and out of school.

Table 5.1   The United Nations Convention on the Rights of the Child (adapted from UNICEF)

Article 1 (Definition of the child)	The Convention defines a 'child' as a person below the age of 18, unless the laws of a particular country set the legal age for adulthood younger.
Article 2 (Non-discrimination)	The Convention applies to all children, whatever their race, religion or abilities.
Article 3 (Best interests of the child)	The best interests of children must be the primary concern in making decisions that may affect them.
Article 4 (Protection of rights)	Governments have a responsibility to take all available measures to make sure children's rights are respected, protected and fulfilled.
Article 12 (Respect for the views of the child)	When adults are making decisions that affect children, children have the right to say what they think should happen and have their opinions taken into account.
Article 13 (Freedom of expression)	Children have the right to get and share information, as long as the information is not damaging to them or others. In exercising the right to freedom of expression, children have the responsibility to also respect the rights, freedoms and reputations of others.
Article 14 (Freedom of thought, conscience and religion)	Children have the right to think and believe what they want and to practise their religion, as long as they are not stopping other people from enjoying their rights. Parents should help guide their children in these matters. The Convention respects the rights and duties of parents in providing religious and moral guidance to their children.
Article 19 (Protection from all forms of violence)	Children have the right to be protected from being hurt and mistreated, physically or mentally. Governments should ensure that children are properly cared for and protect them from violence, abuse and neglect by their parents, or anyone else who looks after them. In terms of discipline, the Convention does not specify what forms of punishment parents should use.
Article 23 (Children with disabilities)	Children who have any kind of disability have the right to special care and support, as well as all the rights in the Convention, so that they can live full and independent lives.
Article 28 (Right to education)	All children have the right to a primary education, which should be free. Wealthy countries should help poorer countries achieve this right. Discipline in schools should respect children's dignity. For children to benefit from education, schools must be run in an orderly way – without the use of violence. Any form of school discipline should take into account the child's human dignity. Therefore, governments must ensure that school administrators review their discipline policies and eliminate any discipline practices involving physical or mental violence, abuse or neglect. The Convention places a high value on education. Young people should be encouraged to reach the highest level of education of which they are capable.

(Continued)

Table 5.1   (Continued)

Article 29 (Goals of education)	Children's education should develop each child's personality, talents and abilities to the fullest. It should encourage children to respect others, human rights and their own and other cultures. It should also help them learn to live peacefully, protect the environment and respect other people.
Article 30 (Children of minorities/indigenous groups)	Minority or indigenous children have the right to learn about and practice their own culture, language and religion.
Article 31 (Leisure, play and culture)	Children have the right to relax and play, and to join in a wide range of cultural, artistic and other recreational activities.
Article 34 (Sexual exploitation)	Governments should protect children from all forms of sexual exploitation and abuse. This provision in the Convention is augmented by the Optional Protocol on the sale of children, child prostitution and child pornography.
Article 36 (Other forms of exploitation)	Children should be protected from any activity that takes advantage of them or could harm their welfare and development.
Article 42 (Knowledge of rights)	Governments must actively work to make sure children and adults know about the Convention.

CASE STUDY

UNICEF works with schools in the UK to create safe and inspiring places to learn, where children are respected, their talents are nurtured and they are able to thrive. The Rights Respecting Schools Award embeds these values in daily school life and gives children the best chance to lead happy, healthy lives and to be responsible, active citizens.

Using the UN Convention on the Rights of the Child (UNCRC) as a guide, many UK schools bring the rights of children to the centre of education. In the UK, 1.5 million children go to a Rights Respecting School and more than 4000 schools in the country are working towards the award. Schools work with us on a journey to become fully Rights Respecting. The Award recognises a school's achievement in putting the United Nations Convention on the Rights of the Child into practice within the school and beyond.

There are four standards which must be achieved in the Rights Respecting School Award:

Standard A: Rights-respecting values underpin leadership and management

The best interests of the child are a top priority in all actions. Leaders are committed to placing the values and principles of the UN Convention on the Rights of the Child at the heart of all policies and practice.

Standard B: The whole school community learns about the UN Convention on the Rights of the Child

The Convention is made known to children and adults. Young people and adults use this shared understanding to work for global justice and sustainable living.

Standard C: The school has a rights-respecting ethos

Young people and adults collaborate to develop and maintain a rights-respecting school community, based on the UN Convention on the Rights of the Child, in all areas and in all aspects of school life.

Standard D: Children and young people are empowered to become active citizens and learners

Every child has the right to say what they think in all matters affecting them and to have their views taken seriously. Young people develop the confidence, through their experience of an inclusive rights-respecting school community, to play an active role in their own learning and to speak and act for the rights of all to be respected locally and globally.

Full details of Rights Respecting Schools can be found at UNICEF (see Bibliography).

Protecting trainees and early career teachers

In this chapter, we have made a strong claim for the well-being of both children and teachers. In fact, well-being always has an external dimension to it (McLeod and Wright, 2015). In the case of mental health, for instance, this is seen as a product of the interaction between teachers, children and the wider community: that is to say, the mental health of teachers as well as pupils. The concept of duty of care to both pupils and staff is very important for leaders in schools. It is enshrined in the second part of the Teachers' Standards:

Teachers uphold public trust in the profession and maintain high standards of ethics and behaviour, within and outside school, by:

- treating pupils with dignity, building relationships rooted in mutual respect, and at all times observing proper boundaries appropriate to a teacher's professional position
- having regard for the need to safeguard pupils' well-being, in accordance with statutory provisions
- showing tolerance of and respect for the rights of others, not undermining fundamental British values including democracy, the rule of law, individual liberty and mutual respect, and tolerance of those with different faiths and beliefs
- ensuring that personal beliefs are not expressed in ways which exploit pupils' vulnerability or might lead them to break the law.

(DfE, 2014)

We believe that new and trainee teachers are particularly vulnerable and therefore they have a right to high quality professional development in their career. It can be argued that having a 'mentor' is really not enough when there is a need for supervision that considers the professional and emotional needs of the teacher. Many newly qualified teachers in the UK explain that their first year working in teaching is the most difficult year because of the high levels of accountability and workload in schools. Listening to teachers, and providing them with knowledge, skills and emotional support, is just as important as listening to children.

Chapter summary

- The quality of relationships (connectedness), personal and professional control (autonomy) and ultimately personal growth (self-actualisation) are at the heart of well-being for both young people and their teachers.
- How can we expect to develop the well-being of pupils if we don't pay equal attention to that of their teachers?
- Of course, pupils are still young and in their formative years, but pupils only lack the experiences that are eventually reflected in the adult concerns and worries later in life.
- Teachers are dealing with their own pressures as well as the challenges of their pupils, often in a pressure-cooker atmosphere of accountability.

- Roberts-Holmes and Bradbury (2016) explain that current approaches to education in the early years in England are having a detrimental effect on both children and teachers. They describe the 'datification of early years' education'.
- In law, employers have a duty of care to their employees, which means that they should take all steps that are reasonably possible to ensure their health, safety and well-being (Advisory, Conciliation and Arbitration Service [ACAS], 2017).
- The 'standard of care' expected of a teacher was held to be that of a person exhibiting the responsible mental qualities of a prudent parent in the circumstances of school, rather than home life.
- Banyard et al. (2017) suggest that good family and care networks, opportunities for developing meaning making, and a voice in their learning all provide ways of coping and achieving high-quality outcomes both in and out of school.
- Legally, employers must abide by relevant health and safety and employment laws, as well as by the common law duty of care.
- We argue for a development in school safeguarding to engage, motivate and empower children and young people to have a strong voice, with appropriate knowledge. Knowledge, control and engagement in safeguarding empowers children and young people (Khan, 2016).
- Children have a right to be safe, healthy and well; and to be able to speak up and to be listened to and acted upon if things are not right.
- Abuse is a form of maltreatment of a child. Somebody may abuse or neglect a child by inflicting harm or by failing to act to prevent harm. Children may be abused in a family or in an institutional or community setting by those known to them or, more rarely, by others (e.g., via the Internet). They may be abused by an adult or adults or by another child or children.

Further reading

National Foundation for Educational Research (NFER) (2016) *Engaging Teachers: NFER Analysis of Teacher Retention*. Windsor: NFER. Available at: http://www. nfer.ac.uk/publications/LFSB01/LFSB01.pdf (accessed 31 December 2017).
This provides a detailed analysis of the reasons why teachers stay in and leave the profession. It provides some suggestions for developing well-being in teachers.

United Nations Children's Fund (UNICEF) 'Rights Respecting Schools: Putting Children's Rights at the Heart of Schools'. Available at: http://www.unicef.org. uk/rights-respecting-schools/ (accessed 31 December 2017).
Full details of Rights Respecting Schools can be found here.

United Nations Children's Fund (UNICEF) (2017) United Nations Convention for the Rights of the Child. Available at: http://www.unicef.org.uk/what-we-do/un-convention-child-rights/ (accessed 31 December 2017).
In our view, a formidable statement of the values that should underpin a civilised society's approach to children and childhood.

Bibliography

Advisory, Conciliation and Arbitration Service (ACAS) (2017) Available at: http://www.acas.org.uk/index.aspx?articleid=3751 (accessed May 2017).

Baynard, V., Hamby, S. and Grych, J. (2017) 'Health effects of adverse childhood events: Identifying promising protective factors at the intersection of mental and physical well-being', *Child Abuse and Neglect*, 65: 88–98.

Briggs, M.K., Akos, P., Czyszczon, G. and Eldridge, A. (2011) 'Assessing and promoting spiritual wellness as a protective factor in secondary schools', *Counseling and Values*, 55 (2): 171–84.

Department for Education (DfE) (2014) *Teachers' Standards*. London: DfE. Available at: http://www.gov.uk/government/uploads/system/uploads/attach ment_data/file/283566/Teachers_standard_information.pdf (accessed May 2017).

Department for Education (DfE) (2016) *Keeping Children Safe in Education*. London: HMSO. Available at: http://www.gov.uk (accessed May 2017).

Department for Education (DfE) (2017) Educate Against Hate. Available at: http://educateagainsthate.com/teachers/why-is-extremism-relevant-to-me-as-a-teacher (accessed May 2017).

Detrick, S. (1999) *A Commentary on the United Nations Convention on the Rights of the Child*. Leiden: Martinus Nijhoff Publishers.

Donaldson Feilder, E. and Podro, S. (2012) *The Future of Health and Wellbeing in the Workplace*. London: ACAS.

Foster, D. (2018) 'Teacher recruitment and retention in England', House of Commons, Library Briefing Paper, No. 7222, 19 January.

Khan, J. (2016) 'Any child can be sexually exploited, whether they fit the stereotypes or not', *The Guardian*, 4 April. Available at: http://www.theguardian.com/social-care-network/2016/apr/04/child-sexual-exploitation-stereotypes-rotherham (accessed 31 December 2017).

Knaus, C. (2017) 'Catholic Church doesn't understand toll of child abuse, says US priest', *The Guardian*, 7 February. Available at: http://www.theguardian.com/australia-news/2017/feb/07/catholic-church-doesnt-understand-toll-of-child-sexual-abuse-says-us-priest (accessed).

League of Nations (2009 [1924]) *Geneva Declaration of the Rights of the Child*, 26 September 1924.

Leicestershire and Rutland Safeguarding Children Board (2015) *Report: 2015 Schools Safeguarding Survey*. Glenfield: Leicestershire and Rutland Safeguarding Children Board. Available at: http://lrsb.org.uk/uploads/the-2015-schools-safeguarding-survey-(rutland).pdf (accessed 30 May 2017).

Lynch, S. (2016) *Engaging Teachers: NFER Analysis of Teacher Retention.* Windsor: National Foundation for Educational Research (NFER).

McLeod, J. and Wright, K. (2015) 'Inventing youth wellbeing', in K. Wright and J. McLeod (eds), *Rethinking Youth Wellbeing: Critical Perspectives.* Singapore: Springer.

National Union of Teachers (NUT) (2012) *NUT Notes 2012–13: Education, the Law and You.* London and NUT Other Regional Offices: NUT. Available at: http://www.teachers.org.uk/files/the-law-and-you--8251-.pdf (accessed May 2017).

National Union of Teachers (NUT) (2014) *Teachers' Working Time and Duties: An NUT Guide.* Available at: https://www.teachers.org.uk/files/workload-a5-2014--9586-.pdf (accessed 27 May 2018).

Roberts-Holmes, G. and Bradbury, A. (2016) 'Governance, accountability and the datafication of early years education in England', *British Educational Research Journal*, 42 (4): 600–13.

Rousseau, J.-J. (1991 [1762]) *Emile, or On Education.* London: Penguin.

Save the Children's Resource Centre. Available at: https://resourcecentre.savethe children.net/our-thematic-areas/cross-thematic-areas/child-participation (accessed 31 December 2017).

Treseder, P. and Smith, P.G. (1997) *Empowering Children & Young People: Training Manual.* London: Save the Children.

United Nations Children's Fund (UNICEF) (2017) 'Rights Respecting Schools: Putting Children's Rights at the Heart of Schools'. Available at: http://www. unicef.org.uk/rights-respecting-schools/ (accessed 31 December 2017).

Wiley, D.C. and Cory, A.C. (2013) *Encyclopedia of School Health.* London: Sage.

6

PROFESSIONAL ENGAGEMENT

Chapter guide

In this chapter, you will learn about:

- Engagement, motivation and empowerment in teachers
- Building a culture of engagement
- Challenge, interest and self-determination
- Strategies for engaging teachers: from training to early career teachers

What is the difference between engagement and motivation of teachers? We believe that this partly defines the identity of the teacher as a professional. Being engaged in teaching and learning means that the teacher is moving beyond the application of teaching strategies to take ownership of their own professional learning and the outcomes of the pupils in their classes. Intrinsic and extrinsic motivation of teachers is explored explicitly. We come back to a resonant theme: Why, despite all the challenges, do many teachers continue to commit themselves to the profession?

Intrinsic motivation of teachers is explored at the level of teacher interests in respect of self-actualisation, connectedness and autonomy. Recent models of self-determination (Deci and Ryan, 2008) are used to explain teacher interests and motivation. These may be different for the trainee, newly qualified and more experienced teachers. Case studies of teachers at different stages of their career are used to illustrate teacher interests, motivation and engagement. Whilst praise for learners in the classroom is seen to be central to the development of behaviour for learning, the role of praise for teachers is less well explored. Indeed, we believe that the ability of teachers both to give and receive praise amongst themselves and to themselves is central to creating a positive, sustaining, emotional and professional climate in school.

REFLECTION POINT

Every teacher has good days and bad days

Make a list of the top aspects of teaching that keep you going, keep you engaged and interest you. Answer the following questions to help you reflect on what keeps you going in teaching.

You can choose the top 10 aspects yourself or you might find it useful to rank from 1 (top) to 10, the following aspects:

- Working with other like-minded adults
- Making a difference to individual children (the light-bulb moment)
- Working with children
- Being good at my job/subject
- Having a laugh with colleagues
- Variety in the work of a teacher
- Challenge in my role
- Leading other people
- Work–life balance: Taking regular breaks through the year with school holidays
- Being a creative teacher.

Now, look at your list and consider how often in the school week/year you get the chance to develop this aspect of your role.

Or another way to look at this is to ask yourself which of the aspects of teaching you find energising and which you find energy-sapping.

How can you build in enough opportunities to experience 'energising' aspects of teaching to keep yourself engaged in the role?

In the above reflection activity it is important to recognise that teachers, like all learners, can be motivated and demotivated at different points in their role. Different people respond to situations in different ways. What motivates one person may not motivate another. As a profession, we need to be more aware of what engages teachers if we want to keep them in the profession. Engaged teachers are more likely to stay in the profession (Foster, 2017). But what does it mean to be 'engaged' as a teacher?

Engagement, motivation and empowerment in teachers

Schieb and Karabenick (2011) suggest that teacher engagement, motivation and empowerment are central to their success as teachers. This can be seen in the teacher's sense of self-efficacy (their beliefs about how effective they are). Of course, it is worth questioning the notion of effectiveness. The educational establishment frequently sees teacher effectiveness as being defined on the basis of their ability to engender progress in pupil learning. Coe et al. (2014: 2-3) identify six factors and the strength of evidence of their impact on pupil learning outcomes. It is not the purpose of this book to identify key factors in teacher effectiveness, but, as these factors interact with teacher engagement, motivation and empowerment, they are critiqued below:

1. *Pedagogical content knowledge*: Strong evidence of impact on student outcomes
2. *Quality of instruction*: Strong evidence of impact on student outcomes
3. *Classroom climate*: Moderate evidence of impact on student outcomes
4. *Classroom management*: Moderate evidence of impact on student outcomes
5. *Teacher beliefs*: Some evidence of impact on student outcomes
6. *Professional behaviours*: Some evidence of impact on student outcomes.

Immediately, we should consider the notion of student outcome as this seems to underpin each of the above factors for teacher effectiveness. Coe et al. (2014: 38–9) state that effective teaching is that which leads to enhanced student outcomes. They go on to say that their criterion measure, against which we should validate all other sources of evidence about effectiveness (such as from lesson observation, student ratings, etc.), must always be anchored in direct evidence of valued learning outcomes. They go on to say that success needs to be defined not in terms of teacher mastery of new strategies or the demonstration of preferred behaviours, but in terms of the impact that changed practice has on valued outcomes. However, because teachers work in such varied contexts, there can be no guarantee that any specific approach to teaching will have the desired outcomes for students (ibid.). To interpret this analysis of effective teaching we can say that:

- Effective teaching is that which leads to enhanced student outcomes, but what student outcomes?
- Evidence of effective student outcomes needs to be located in direct evidence of valued learning outcomes; so which methods to gain direct evidence are valid, and what constitutes valued outcomes?

- Given that the varied contexts within which teachers work are critical in effecting outcomes, it seems pertinent to question the desired outcomes of different contexts.

Questioning the nature of effective teaching may seem like a laboured argument and over-analysing the classroom context. But when it comes to judging teacher engagement, motivation and empowerment, what teachers value as student outcomes and the student experience of teaching and learning are critical factors. We argue here that both the nature of educational outcomes and the learning journey for students are critical in teacher engagement and motivation. For instance, we can see student learning as follows:

- **Cognitive:** For example, that based on knowledge of facts and conceptual understanding as often laid out in the school curriculum.
- **Social, emotional and affective:** For example, as evidenced by students' behaviour and motivation, and their ability to demonstrate the so-called 'soft skills' of communication, teamwork and self-reliance – skills, attitudes and abilities often highlighted by future employers and parents as being desirable student outcomes.
- **Physical:** For example, as evidenced in biological factors such as physical health, fitness and childhood growth parameters.
- **Moral, ethical and spiritual:** For example, as are often espoused in the faith-based expectations of schools with an adherence to a particular religious ethos, such as Christianity, Judaism, Islam, Sikism or Hinduism.

We would like to make it very clear that curriculum progression and cognitive growth are, of course, critical to student outcomes. However, there has been perhaps too great a focus given to these elements and less to other less 'measurable' factors like social, emotional, affective, physical, moral, ethical and spiritual dimensions to both the learning journey and student outcomes. This final point is critical, because we believe that the experience of learning is just as important as the student outcomes. The ends do not justify the means: only bad student outcomes come from a bad learning experience. As Guy Claxton (2007: 115) says, 'every time you learn something, you learn something about learning'.

The root of teacher engagement and therefore student progress is in what we value as teachers and learning in both the experience and outcome of learning. Both students and teachers experience motivation from the student and teacher experience of the classroom and classroom outcomes.

There is great evidence to suggest that when both teachers and learners are involved in learning activities and objectives to which they are not committed and do not value, teacher engagement is diminished, and one result of this is the lowering of student outcomes. Hein et al. (2012) explains that teachers' perceptions of their own autonomy can have a dramatic impact on their motivation. The more a teacher feels they can exercise some control and choice in their work, then the more they are intrinsically motivated for their work. It seems entirely credible to suggest that by aligning teaching to their core values, an individual teacher is more likely to enjoy their role. A teacher who is more motivated and enjoys their role is more likely to motivate and teach their classes more successfully. If teachers are developed and recruited on the basis of strong and appropriate values that include a commitment to both student experience and student outcomes, then effective teaching and learning is entirely compatible with a happy and motivated workforce.

This last argument can be further enhanced by a consideration of the link between pupil outcomes and teacher outcomes in terms of emotional well-being. Salter-Jones (2012: 18) quotes the National Institute for Health and Clinical Excellence (NICE, 2008) in identifying that 'the importance of developing positive relationships between pupils and staff is seen as imperative when promoting pupils' emotional well-being' Jennings and Greenberg (2009: 491). Salter-Jones (2012) explains that the way in which teaching staff respond to pupils' social, emotional and behavioural needs is recognised by students as, in part, due to the teachers' own well-being. According to research carried out by Salter-Jones (2012), pupils agreed that the teacher's personal and teaching skills, as well as the quality of the relationships between them and their pupils, are imperative, as these situations provide opportunities for the modelling of appropriate social interactions and interpersonal behaviours that they are trying to encourage. Her view is that 'the teachers' skills will naturally be influenced by their own social and emotional skills, their willingness to engage in the pastoral curriculum and their own emotional well-being' (ibid.: 23). The message here is that just talking about emotional well-being is not enough. Schools need to consider carefully the best way to develop teachers' emotional well-being as teachers need to model this to their pupils. Teachers are not just deliverers of knowledge, they are also very important role models. Pupils, parents and the community look up to teachers because of who they are and how they behave. Of course, some teachers would argue that this level of respect is not always in place in all sectors of the school community, but this does not undermine the argument for teachers as role models.

Teacher well-being is therefore considered to be vital for motivation, engagement and empowerment. Empowering teachers comes from professional freedom. Professional freedom implies both rights and responsibilities. With responsibility comes accountability. The nature of teacher accountability should be carefully considered to ensure that the model of accountability is closely aligned with the appropriate teacher values. Again, we reassert a view of accountability in relation to the quality of both student and teacher experience and outcomes. A school that achieves amazing exam results to the detriment of both student and teacher well-being cannot be judged as being as successful as a school in which both teachers and pupils thrive in an enabling, motivating and frankly happy environment – with great exam results. The student and teacher learning experience is important alongside student and teacher learning outcomes. If these are the reasons why teacher engagement, motivation and empowerment are important, how do we actually achieve this?

Building a culture of engagement

It is worth seeing this question in a very practical way if this is going to be useful for teachers and schools. We have discussed in some depth 'why' engaging both students and teachers is a good thing. The framework in Table 6.1 considers some suggestions.

Table 6.1   How to build a culture of engagement in school

Some questions		Some suggestions	
1.	What does engagement look like in teachers and students?	1.	Teachers and learners are engaged by the degree they attend to, commit to and focus on teaching and learning activities.
2.	What is different between engagement in teachers and students?	2.	Engagement in teachers and students might involve different language and activities, but essentially there is much in common.
3.	What form of leadership encourages engagement in teachers and students?	3.	Leadership for engagement seeks to understand the core values of staff and students and to build a common purpose around these values to develop positive teaching and learning experiences and outcomes.
4.	What is the language of engagement for students and teachers?	4.	Excellent communication is a two-way process. This involves positive language to reinforce effort made by both teachers and students.
5.	Who sets the culture and values of an engaged school and classroom?	5.	All teachers and students have a responsibility to promote praise and positive language. This develops a positive classroom culture. School leaders must emphasise everyone's responsibility.
6.	Who identifies whether a student, teacher or school is engaged?	6.	Ultimately, every teacher and student has an individual responsibility to challenge themselves, to take ownership. Teachers and learners must aim for self-regulated learning.

Some questions	Some suggestions
7. When in a lesson, does the teacher and student demonstrate engagement?	7. Of course, engagement should happen in all aspects of a lesson, but the teacher may take a lead in the lesson. Engagement can be seen in listening, speaking or, indeed, in just thinking and reflecting.
8. When in a student and teacher's lifespan does engagement start?	8. Engagement is central to all learning, from immediately after birth to old age, but we have different interests, motivations and skills.
9. Where and how is engagement developed in a teacher?	9. Engagement in learning for a teacher develops with initial training and, in particular, through their placements, part of high-quality professional development.
10. Where in a classroom and school is engagement created and seen?	10. Engagement can be seen in people, the classroom environment and the general culture of the school: in what teachers and students do, say and see.

Table 6.1 explains what engagement looks like and where it develops in a teachers' career, but how can schools and teachers encourage greater teacher engagement? This can be encapsulated in the diagram in Figure 6.1.

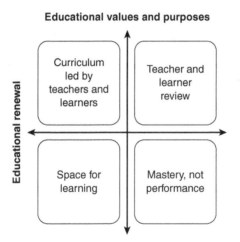

Figure 6.1 Engaging teachers and students in the classroom

Educational values and purposes: At a national level, every country needs to ensure that the professional framework and standards for teachers are led by teachers towards the right educational values and purposes. Driving the profession for political purposes in a direction away from that which most teachers would agree with is a quick way of disengaging and therefore of losing teachers from the profession.

Teacher and learner review: Build a model of teacher accountability led by teachers. Peer evaluation provides freedom for teachers to evaluate success and improve education for learners, but also great responsibility. Only with responsibility can we expect teachers to fully engage with their roles.

Teacher and learner-led curriculum: Build a school curriculum locally devised, implemented and improved by teachers. As teachers in Finland have found, a ten-year curriculum review cycle is challenging, but it does ensure that curriculum aims and objectives strongly align with the values and purposes of teachers.

Teaching and learning renewal: Build a strong culture of professional development, self-review and action research in schools. This echoes Stenhouse's (1975) view of the teacher-researcher leading the school curriculum.

Mastery, not performance: Build a culture of learning rather than a culture of performance. As Dweck (2000) suggests, students and teachers should focus on deeper learning and praising effort, since this encourages a mastery orientation to learning, rather than a performance orientation to learning. Teachers should be judged on educational mastery rather than educational performance.

Space for learning: Teachers and students can be co-creators of knowledge in the classroom, but this requires time and a commitment to taking risks. Not all learning needs to be more discovery based and learner led, but opportunities throughout the week encourage engagement from both teachers and students. It also encourages responsibility for self-regulated learning in students, which should be a focus for education. Likewise, cultivating depth requires trust in teachers and learners. Learning will not be perfect every time, but it will be better with more space for innovation and creativity.

Taking this again to a very practical level, here are ten things that teachers and learners can do in school to encourage engagement:

1. Listen to staff by committing to a proper and authentic staff liaison committee.
2. Plan for teachers to have time to share ideas and plan together.
3. Expect all teachers to act as mentors and coaches for each other as well as for new entrants to the profession.
4. Provide opportunities for staff to be creative in their roles, often by providing opportunities and people from outside the profession as stimulus.

5. Build a professional development library for staff.
6. Invite students to lead aspects of school professional development: feedback from learners on teaching can be very powerful.
7. Work with other people in a lesson study or learning set group to address a challenge in school: involving both teachers and learners and maybe even parents in this can be a great way to engage people.
8. Write case studies of learning linked to curriculum development, working with a local university for support, expertise and interest.
9. Make links with schools in your area, your local university and international schools overseas.
10. Give the opportunity to staff to study and teach abroad on secondment and sabbatical, providing that they bring these ideas back into school.

Of course, we could go further in this, but you will start to recognise some areas that schools have already established to engage teachers and learners. We argue that these must be more than tokenistic gestures so as to establish long-term commitment to teachers. On the other hand, teachers must then commit to engagement, as many already do in school. Engagement can take many forms. Teacher engagement can also be a question of degree. Does it always have to be a deep and almost esoteric experience? Schmidt et al. articulate this deep level of engagement in the classroom as follows:

- intense concentration on the task at hand;
- a deep sense of involvement and merging of action and awareness;
- a sense of control over one's actions in dealing with the task at hand;
- enjoyment or interest in the activity; and
- a distorted sense of time (usually that time has passed very quickly). (2014: 379)

They explain that the factors that influence anyone – including those in teaching – in this deep level of engagement vary between individuals, according to age, gender, ethnicity and geography. However, there are some common conditions that encourage 'flow' in the classroom:

- Engagement in activity chosen for its own sake
- Perceived challenges of the task at hand that are relatively high and in balance with one's perceived skills
- Clear proximal goals that are regarded as important
- Immediate feedback indicating one's success at meeting these goals
- Highly focused, rather than divided or scattered, attention.

Part of the issue in engagement is to ensure an appropriate balance between learner skills and learning challenge. Schmidt et al. (ibid.) encapsulate this in the model in Figure 6.2.

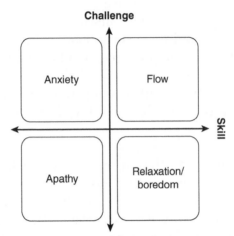

Figure 6.2 The relationship between challenge and skill in developing engagement (Reprinted from International Encyclopedia of Education, Schmidt, J., Flow in Education, 605–611, (2010), with permission from Elsevier)

Challenge in any school activity needs to be balanced with an understanding of the current level of skill. This is equally true of teachers in school. Where there is insufficient challenge, this can lead to apathy and boredom – probably a reason why teachers leave one school to go and find a job in another. But when the challenge is increased, a lack of skill – and we would include capacity – can lead to anxiety. Having the skills to complete a teaching task can sometimes be seen as a group attribute, rather than just a personal one. The point about a teacher's 'capacity' is very important. Having the skills but not the time to build challenge into the teacher role can lead to that feeling we have probably all felt at some point: 'This is great but I just don't know how I'm going to get this done in the time that I've got.' This is why we argued for space, depth and mastery in learning. Giving teachers activities to do that are interesting and challenging but not the time or resources to accomplish them will lead to disengagement, not engagement.

Developing 'engaged' teachers is therefore about looking at the interests of teachers, but building challenge and capacity into their roles. This can be explained through the work of Ryan and Deci (2000) on self-determination.

Challenge, interest and self-determination

Schmidt et al. (2014) identify environment as a significant opportunity for developing engagement or, more particularly, 'flow'. Here, we also return to those factors that engage and interest teachers. At the start of this chapter, we suggested interest in a teacher's subject and a genuine commitment to teaching and student outcomes as reasons for staying in the profession. There is a happy intersection between the factors that encourage 'flow' in students and those that encourage 'flow' in teachers. Schmidt et al. (2014) explain that a more didactic teaching style often leads to a less involved and less engaged student experience. However, a teaching approach that emphasises scaffolding of learning should be based on a good balance between learner needs and degree of challenge in a learning activity. Add into this happy marriage the opportunity to experiment with different approaches to teaching supports, both renewal in teaching as well as varying the learning landscape. This is best achieved with the aid of colleagues to provide professional support: always social, emotional and physical. Teaching can be a physically demanding activity, energy-sapping and basically hard to do across a day, a week and a year. So, having a colleague to coach teachers in new approaches to teaching is essential. There is also a uniquely important social dimension to working with and supporting colleagues.

Teaching and learning are also uniquely connected. You can't really teach without learners. So, when there are opportunities to experiment and develop different forms of teaching, it can only be done with the involvement and, we would argue, conscious awareness of the learners. Teachers can feel defensive about sharing vulnerability with learning when they are trying something new in the classroom. If teaching and learning is a joint enterprise, then students have as much responsibility as teachers do to make new teaching approaches work. New teaching and new learning is a joint enterprise, in which both teachers and students take risks to develop something more interesting. The difficulty here is that new approaches can result in a sense of uncertainty and anxiety. This is the classic 'U shape' of change, with things feeling worse when a new approach is adopted in any setting. Whilst we are keen not to adopt the latest educational 'fad', the concepts of 'resilience' and 'grit' can be useful to support emotional stability caused by uncertainty when the teacher and learner tries something new in the classroom.

If we commit to new approaches to teaching and learning in order to challenge both teachers and learners, we must learn to accept that uncertainty will be part of our classroom lives. Zero challenge risks zero engagement and motivation for learning in both teachers and students. Always resting on the 'tried-and-tested' approaches risks engendering boredom and a risk-averse approach, which emphasises performance rather than mastery in the classroom. The diagram in Figure 6.3 explains something of the social and emotional challenges that teachers and students have when developing new approaches to teaching and learning.

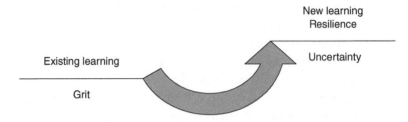

Figure 6.3 The relationship between learning, uncertainty and perseverance (adapted from Duckworth 2016)

This explains that new approaches to learning move through a stage of uncertainty for both teachers and learners. Both need determination to overcome this uncertainty. This is often characterised as 'grit' (Duckworth, 2016). Tenacity and perseverance, in this case for learning, means seeing through what you started and overcoming temporary obstacles with a problem-solving mentality. Longer-term obstacles can be seen as a sequence of shorter-term challenges to be understood and addressed. Problem-solving, in this case, means considering various options and discovering some new approaches to overcoming barriers to learning. This is the perfect antidote to some of the very instrumental, atomistic approaches to teaching and learning in the last 20 years. Learning with uncertainty means persevering and actively trying to resolve the issues that are preventing completion of a task. Passive, learned helplessness means people sit back and wait to be told what to do. Of course, we mean that this applies to teachers as well as students. Teachers need challenge as much as students, if they are to be genuinely engaged in their role. But they must be given the space and responsibility to consider the best way to overcome all elements of the challenge – this includes having enough time to plan, pilot and evaluate new ways of teaching and learning.

CASE STUDY

A primary school has decided amongst the senior management team that the teaching of mathematics across the school is not progressing in the way that was hoped. Test results at the end of the year are starting to take a downward turn. This only mirrors what the head teacher felt from lesson observations she had carried out throughout the year.

You have been contacted by a rep from an international publisher about a new approach to maths teaching from Eastern Europe. Whilst the scheme is quite expensive, it looks promising and you have seen some demonstration lessons in another school. The head of that school is full of praise for the new approach: 'It will definitely work in your school!'
What next and why?

Option 1: Do you take the plunge and buy the new scheme along with the training package to implement the new mathematics scheme?

Option 2: Do you run a pilot of the scheme in selected classes to identify how you would or could implement the scheme in your school?

Why does an evidence-based approach to teaching reap rewards?

Teachers recognise that every school is different and that what works for one school many not work in another. One of the first challenges of a teacher is to understand their local context and to ascertain how they can adapt to it. A good leader will help teachers through their induction to the school to fully understand both the community and school variables that will influence the implementation of a new approach to teaching and learning. This understanding will help teachers to adjust the implementation of new approaches to teaching and learning so that they are sensitive to the particular influences on the curriculum. A pilot period to evaluate, adapt and tweak approaches to teaching and learning surely makes sense. This alone is an excellent example of teachers taking innovations and adapting them to the local context. Teachers making choices that will positively impact on learning demonstrates engagement.

Choice, the exercise of control and agency are elements of Deci and Ryan's (2008) theory of self-determination. Connecting with other teachers is also critical for engaged teachers. The social dimension to teaching has a strong protective aspect for teachers. It helps them make sense of their work. It helps them to share and defuse concerns about their work. Finally, the notion of growth seems to be central to teacher engagement. It reflects development through adversity (grit) and genuine joy of teaching implied in Schmidt et al.'s (2014) analysis of flow in education. A central argument of this book is that self-determination is as important for teachers as it is for students.

Strategies for engaging teachers: From training to early career teachers

Latterly, we have seen the importance of understanding school contexts when adapting and implementing new approaches to teaching and learning in school. In order to analyse this challenge, we suggest the following matrix:

Above: School leadership and wider groups that might dictate how teachers are engaged.

Within: Factors within the teachers, such as values, interests and professional biography – all part of a teacher's identity.

Below: The learners, how they behave and their particular cultures – any one of which might be in opposition to that of the teacher.

Around: The community – as for children, how they behave, their values and interests.

Just as learners have an identity, so do teachers. This develops from experiences such as having themselves been a student in school and through their wider family and professional biography. In Finland, teacher training includes significant reflection on the trainee teacher's own learning biography, since this will have a significant impact on how they teach and also learn as a professional (see Lortie's concept of an 'apprenticeship of observation'; 1977). For instance, we have already identified a difference in the role that leaders have in leading engagement through teachers, as opposed to doing the teaching themselves. Leaders develop capacity for teachers to engage with and further develop their own solutions in the classroom. Deci and Ryan's (2008) focus on connecting teachers to develop self-determination in school can be translated into the role of teacher leaders to connect their new teachers with experienced teachers. Whilst this can be a little forced, 'buddying' new and training teachers with teachers recently having moved from this stage themselves provides teachers with the chance to discuss coping and resilience at an early stage of their career. Developing networks of mentors and coaches for aspiring school leaders also creates authentic opportunities for teachers to challenge themselves to develop leadership skills. Different people may need different support at different stages, for instance early career teachers as opposed to those later in their careers. A very interesting analysis of teachers' professional lives was carried out by Day et al. (2006). Their research suggested the following stages in the professional lives of teachers.

Professional life phase 0–3 years: Commitment – Support and challenge

Subgroups:

a.   Developing sense of efficacy; *or*
b.   Reduced sense of efficacy

Professional life phase 4–7 years: Identity and efficacy in the classroom

Subgroups:

a.   Sustaining a strong sense of identity, self-efficacy and effectiveness; *or*
b.   Sustaining identity, efficacy and effectiveness; *or*
c.   Identity, efficacy and effectiveness at risk

Professional life phase 8–15 years: Managing changes in role and identity – Growing tensions and transitions

Subgroups:

a.   Sustained engagement; *or*
b.   Detachment/loss of motivation

Professional life phase 16–23 years: Work–life tensions – Challenges to motivation and commitment

Subgroups:

a.   Further career advancement and good results have led to increased motivation/commitment; *or*
b.   Sustained motivation, commitment and effectiveness; *or*
c.   Workload/managing competing tensions/career stagnation have led to decreased motivation, commitment and effectiveness

Professional life phase 24–30 years: Challenges to sustaining motivation

Subgroups:

a.   Sustained a strong sense of motivation and commitment; *or*
b.   Holding on but losing motivation

Professional life phase 31+: Sustaining/declining motivation, ability to cope with change, looking to retire

Subgroups:

a. Maintaining commitment; *or*
b. Tired and trapped

Day et al. (2006: 612)

REFLECTION POINT

Day et al.'s (2006) analysis of teachers' professional lives indicates some subgroups in terms of how they are coping or thriving at that particular stage of their career:

- Consider the stage at which you are at the moment.
- Reflect on the subgroups: Which ones best represents your professional life to this date?
- In particular, how has your motivation and commitment changed during your career as a teacher?

Whilst consideration of strategies to support all teachers is beyond the scope of this book, below we make some practical suggestions for trainee and early career teachers to sustain their engagement in teaching.

Professional life phase 0–3 years: Commitment – Support and challenge

The phrase 'just about managing' could easily be deployed for many teachers in their training and early career phase as teachers. But so many trainees and new teachers are so different that it would not be right to label all teachers as the same and therefore needing similar approaches to sustain their motivation. Day et al.'s (2006) analysis of a sense of efficacy is interesting here. It suggests that trainee and newly qualified teachers need positive feedback to reinforce their professional self-concept in terms of their effectiveness. However, it is essential that the work of crafting a teacher's identity with strong values must carry on through their early career. Whilst a teacher must adapt to their school, the school must also adapt to the teacher. Opportunities to reinforce and refine their identity as a teacher are critical to maintaining motivation and engagement.

Professional life phase 4–7 years: Identity and efficacy in classroom

If a sense of efficacy in the first few years of their training is important, then a growing need to come back to their core values, purpose and identity seems to be a need for many teachers. In England, approximately 30 per cent of teachers leave the profession within five years. Is this because by the fourth or fifth year of their career, the values and purpose that drove them to enter the profession have been dislodged by a weariness born of too great a workload and too little consideration of their professional identity? At this point, it would be useful to develop opportunities to connect and seek experiences to reinforce professional identity so that there is a sense of growth. We mentioned before that short-term opportunities to work in international schools or as a teacher educator in a local university could be really important ways of sustaining teacher engagement through sabbaticals and secondments.

Teacher engagement is as important as student engagement. For the learning journey and learning outcomes to be achieved, a good education needs to be built on strong core values and educational purposes in order to maintain teacher engagement. This is important throughout the early stages of a teachers' career.

Chapter summary

- Teacher engagement, motivation and empowerment are central to their success as teachers.
- Both the nature of educational outcomes and the learning journey for students are critical in teacher engagement and motivation.
- Curriculum progression and cognitive growth are, of course, critical to student outcomes. But there has been perhaps too great a focus given to these elements and less to other, less 'measurable', factors like social, emotional, affective, physical, moral, ethical and spiritual dimensions to both the learning journey and student outcomes.
- The experience of learning is just as important as the student outcomes.
- The following factors should be considered in developing teacher engagement:
    - educational values and purposes
    - teacher and learner review
    - teacher and learner-led curriculum
    - teaching and learning renewal
    - mastery not performance
    - space for learning.

- Challenge in any school activity needs to be balanced with an understanding of the current level of skill. This is equally true of teachers in school. Where there is insufficient challenge, this can lead to apathy and boredom.
- Learning with uncertainty means persevering and actively trying to resolve the issues that are preventing the completion of a task. This is equally the case for teachers as it is for students.
- Passive, learned helplessness means that people sit back and wait to be told what to do.
- Different people may need different support at different stages, for instance as early career teachers as opposed to those later in their careers.
- It is essential that the work of crafting a teacher's identity with strong values must carry this work on throughout their early career. Whilst a teacher must adapt to their school, the school must also adapt to the teacher.
- Opportunities to reinforce and refine their identity as a teacher are critical to maintaining motivation and engagement.

Further reading

Day, C.W., Kington, A., Stobart, G. and Sammons, P. (2006) 'The personal and professional selves of teachers: Stable and unstable identities', *British Educational Research Journal*, 32 (4): 601–16.
This explains the experiences of teachers across their careers. Their identities change in response to the different stages of their career.

Salter-Jones, E. (2012) 'Promoting the emotional well-being of teaching staff in secondary schools', *Educational & Child Psychology*, 29 (4): 18–31.
How do we support teachers in school? This article suggests some ideas that are relevant and contribute to the debate.

Schmidt, J.A., Shernoff, D.J., and Csikszentmihalyi, M. (2007) 'Individual and situational factors related to the experience of flow in adolescence: A multilevel approach', in A.D. Ong and M. van Dulmen (eds), *The Handbook of Methods in Positive Psychology*. Oxford: Oxford University Press.
This is an excellent articulation of the concept of 'flow' and how to support learning that is meaningful for the child.

Bibliography

Claxton, G. (2007) Expanding young people's capacity to learn. *British Journal of Educational Studies*, 55 (2): 115–34.
Coe, R., Aloisi, C., Higgins, S. and Major, L.E. (2014) *What Makes Great Teaching? Review of the Underpinning Research*. Durham and London: Centre for Evaluation and Monitoring (CEM), Durham University, and The Sutton Trust.

Day, C.W., Kington, A., Stobart, G. and Sammons, P. (2006) 'The personal and professional selves of teachers: Stable and unstable identities', *British Educational Research Journal*, 32 (4): 601–16.

Deci, E.L. and Ryan, R.M. (2008) 'Facilitating optimal motivation and psychological well-being across life's domains', *Canadian Psychology*, 49 (1): 14–23.

Dickinson, L. (1995) 'Autonomy and motivation: A literature review', *System*, 23 (2): 165–74.

Duckworth, A. (2016) *Grit: The Power of Passion and Perseverance*. New York: Simon & Schuster.

Dweck, C.S. (2000) *Self-Theories: Their Role in Motivation, Personality, and Development*. London: Psychology Press.

Foster, D. (2017) 'Teacher recruitment and retention in England', House of Commons, Library Briefing Paper, No. 7222, 12 June.

Hein, V. et al. (2012) The relationship between teaching styles and motivation to teach among physical education teachers. *Journal of Sports Science & Medicine*, 11 (1): 123.

Jennings, P.A. and Greenberg, M.T. (2009) The prosocial classroom: Teacher social and emotional competence in relation to student and classroom outcomes. *Review of Educational Research*, 79 (1): 491–525.

Lortie, D.C. (1977) *Schoolteacher: A Sociological Study*. Chicago, IL: University of Chicago Press.

National Institute for Health and Clinical Excellence (NICE) (2008) *Promoting Children's Social and Emotional Well-Being in Primary Education*. NICE Public Health Guidance 12.

Ryan, R.M. and Deci, E.L. (2000) 'Self-determination theory and the facilitation of intrinsic motivation, social development, and well-being', *American Psychologist*, 55 (1): 68–78.

Salter-Jones, E. (2012) 'Promoting the emotional well-being of teaching staff in secondary schools', *Educational & Child Psychology*, 29 (4): 18–31.

Schieb, L.J. and Karabenick, S.A. (2011) 'Motivation and teacher PD resource categories. *Teacher Motivation and Professional Development: A Guide to Resources*. Math and Science Partnership – Motivation Assessment Program, University of Michigan, Ann Arbor, MI.

Schmidt, J. A. (2010) 'Flow in education', in P. Peterson, R. Tierney, E. Baker and B. McGaw (eds), *International Encyclopedia of Education*. Oxford: Elsevier Ltd. DOI: 10.1016/B978-0-08-044894-7.00608-4

Schmidt, J.A., Shernoff, D.J. and Csikszentmihalyi, M. (2014) 'Individual and situational factors related to the experience of flow in adolescence', in M. Csikszentmihalyi, *Applications of Flow in Human Development and Education: The Collected Works of Mihaly Csikszentmihalyi*. Dodrecht: Springer.

Stenhouse, L. (1975) *An Introduction to Curriculum Research and Development*. London: Heinemann.

7

MOTIVATING ALL LEARNERS

Chapter guide

In this chapter, you will learn about:

- The learner as an individual and the importance of valuing this individuality

- The academic needs of the learner and how to differentiate effectively

- The importance of the emotional and pastoral needs of the learner

- The potential sociocultural contexts of the learner and how these link to inclusion

In Chapter 3, we outlined a number of theoretical approaches to motivation and explored ways of using these in everyday classroom practice. This chapter builds on this theoretical underpinning, but with a specific focus on motivating *all* pupils. We will explore how learners are profiled and identified as members of particular 'targeted groups' within the UK education system, signposting key educational topics such as inclusion, differentiation and personalisation. We will consider how learners' academic and pastoral needs can influence their educational experiences, with a particular focus on those learners identified as 'higher ability'. We will also explore some possible sociocultural contexts of learners, briefly considering how ethnicity and social class can interact with the classroom environment.

What do we mean by *all* pupils?

It could be seen as ambitious to aim to motivate *all* of our learners and to cater for *all* of their individual needs. However, it is this culture of high expectations and ambition that, for us, characterises the teaching profession. In the UK, the Teachers' Standards, which all trainee teachers have to meet (in their training year, induction year and throughout the rest of their career as a qualified teacher), explicitly state that teachers must 'adapt teaching to respond to the strengths and needs of all pupils' (Department for Education (DfE), 2011). Despite this statutory requirement, there is debate in some quarters about how far teachers can be expected to diverge for the individual needs of their learners and what this should entail. Graham (2017) identifies a rise in the prevalence and visibility of the 'neo-traditional' teacher in England, who sees differentiation as unnecessary. She explains that:

> The neo-traditional teacher favours teacher-centred instruction, deplores inclusion and differentiation, and promotes strict whole-school 'no excuses' discipline policies modelled on an extreme interpretation of behaviourism. (Ibid.: 3)

In Chapter 4 we explored how positive learner behaviours can be encouraged, and we set out our vision for a mutually respectful, equitable relationship between teachers and their learners. Later, in Chapter 10, we will go even further than this and explore how the teacher–learner relationship can become truly empowering, with the learner afforded increasing agency and autonomy without the authority of the teacher being compromised. Having taught in a variety of educational settings between us, we have never found it necessary to suppress the learner in the classroom in order to manage behaviour. In fact, both of us have found that even learners who are labelled as disruptive across the school can be re-engaged with the school community and the curriculum when teachers establish and maintain high-quality, professional relationships with them. In a systematic literature review, Quinn cautiously concluded that positive teacher–learner relationships are likely to 'benefit students displaying overt signs of low engagement and simultaneously facilitate students' psychological engagement' (2017: 378), a finding that matches our experiences in education. We passionately believe that inclusion and differentiation are key aspects of the role of the teacher.

The cognitive abilities of the learner

The early stages of a teaching career can be very difficult, with trainee teachers experiencing a loss of leisure time and developing a changing professional identity, which can be unsettling. As a result of this, some aspects of educational thought are distilled into 'tips-for-teachers' approaches that can be over-simplified, over-generalised and arguably disempowering for those teachers who come to rely on them over their own forms of professional knowledge.

Whilst we would never dismiss the experiential knowledge that teachers acquire from their classroom practice and subsequently share with one another, we seek to signpost the dangers of superficial engagement with such issues as cognitive ability, ethnicity, gender and social class. Although it is important to be clear and straightforward when writing about teaching strategies, it is also essential to warn that any generalisations made in this chapter are motivated by this desire for clarity as opposed to a belief in learners as homogeneous members of particular groups.

There is nothing wrong with providing straightforward, practical advice for teachers, but there is a danger that this advice can be embraced wholeheartedly without critical thought or understanding of the reasons for its efficacy or potential failure in particular contexts. Learners are individuals just like us. We do not have time to explore concepts such as individual identity or identity performance here, but suffice it to say that, in our view, effective teaching is rooted in a positive relationship with a learner that values their individuality. This valuing of their personal identity contrasts with approaches that see particular students as manifesting particular behaviours due to their social class or cognitive abilities, and therefore recommends a particular approach for dealing with 'these' learners based on these generalised, unevidenced findings. We will draw on empirical research and practical experience in exploring some potential classroom strategies here, but want to be very clear that these are possibilities that should only be used, trialled, evaluated and refined if you deem them suitable for your learners.

CASE STUDY

A trainee teacher wanted to demonstrate effective differentiation for 'higher-ability learners' in the Year 9 mathematics class that they had just started teaching. Using the school's data-tracking system, the trainee teacher compiled a list of all the learners in the group who were identified as 'higher ability' across all subjects by the school. The teacher planned for these learners to finish the task on probability early, and then to use iPads in order to film the progress of other learners in the classroom and to support them in completing their own tasks.

As the first five learners completed their task, the teacher handed them a card that explained that they now needed to collect an iPad from the back of the classroom and then ask other learners questions about their progress, helping them if necessary:

(Continued)

(Continued)

- What potential problems can you envisage with this approach?
- What could have happened next?

The learners, having never been consciously made aware of strategies for meaningfully ascertaining the progress of learners in relation to a particular mathematical topic, awkwardly interrupted the work of other learners in the class by asking them vague questions (e.g., 'Are you okay with the work?'), which were met with similarly imprecise replies (e.g., 'Alright, thanks'). For one learner identified as 'higher ability', who had in the past been treated for social anxiety, the interpersonal demands of this additional task were overwhelming, and they left the room in tears. For another 'higher-ability learner', who had underachieved since the beginning of Key Stage 3 (between the ages of 11 and 14 in England) and rushed through their worksheet quickly but unfortunately inaccurately, the sight of the detailed notes and answers that contradicted his own was discomfiting and he began distracting other learners by encouraging them to take 'selfies' with him using the iPad.

In this instance, the teacher did not cognitively challenge the 'higher-ability learners' effectively. There were a number of issues that you have probably already identified:

- The teacher relied on whole-school data and did not cross-reference this with her own knowledge of the learners' abilities in relation to this particular mathematical topic, meaning that the underachieving learner was not supported in his understanding of the topic and achieved very little during the lesson.
- The teacher expected the 'higher-ability learners' to accurately assess the progress of other learners through questioning without giving them any tools with which to do so.
- The use of the iPads in order to capture this 'progress' in an audio-visual format is not rooted in the final outcome of the lesson, nor does this seem to have any potential future use.
- The teacher did not consider the emotional needs of the learner who had a history of social anxiety. We all make mistakes as teachers, and we should encourage and support our learners in developing social skills: but by planning such a 'high-stakes' task for this learner in terms of social interaction, without explaining this in advance and consulting the learner, meant that a highly visible, negative emotional outburst took place in the classroom, which could have further implications for the teacher's relationship with this particular learner and in terms of the class dynamic afterwards.
- Arguably, the 'higher-ability learners' were not cognitively stretched by the activity and would have benefited from developing a deeper understanding of the topic or moving on to a more challenging but related topic.

As Slee explains, it is important to remember that: 'students enter school with different talents and intellectual capacities, but ability is constructed by schools and is assigned to them through the organisation of schools' (2014: 449). Many schools identify learners as 'lower ability', 'middle ability' or 'higher ability', based on some form of empirical assessment. Teachers are then encouraged to cater to the needs of these 'groups', sometimes with a narrow, fixed view of the learners within them. There is nothing wrong with teachers using broader generalisations in order to help conceptualise the learning needs of individual learners. If this approach helps a teacher to introduce and consolidate relevant learning for different learners, with careful, meaningful and formative assessments enabling them to swiftly decrease or increase the level of challenge as appropriate for that learner, then that is great. However, there is a danger in the explicit labelling of particular learners as possessing particular levels of ability, not least because it inherently relies on a fixed view of intelligence that is critiqued by thinkers such as Dweck (see Chapter 3).

Matthews et al. provide a useful overview of the use of learner labelling in schools:

> While labels conveniently define attributes (e.g., giftedness, specific learning disability or attention deficit hyperactivity disorder) and assist educators in meeting a child's individual needs, excessive emphasis on labels may devalue the child as a person. (2014: 372)

They summarise four key labelling theories that are useful for us to consider as we navigate this tricky topic:

- The theory of the 'halo effect' suggests that learners can be perceived broadly in particular ways based on just one particular characteristic. They give the example of a gifted learner being labelled as confrontational due to a propensity to regularly ask questions. Halo effects can be negative, as in the previous example, or positive, which can in turn have a negative impact if the teacher is unable to recognise the real needs of a learner due to the halo effect.
- The theory of the 'stereotype threat' focuses on the changes that may occur within a learner's performances as a result of their reaction to a stereotype that they wish to avoid being associated with. Matthews et al. (ibid.) exemplify this by referring to some of the stereotypes associated with gender and science, technology, engineering and mathematics (STEM) subjects.
- The 'Pygmalion theory' draws on the concept of the self-fulfilling prophecy, whereby a positive or negative label attached to a learner is reinforced through their experiences and others'

behaviours towards them and becomes reality to a degree. Whereas the Pygmalion effect refers to the positive effects of the self-fulfilling prophecy, the 'golem effect' refers to the effects of a negative self-fulfilling prophecy.

- 'Labelling theory' asserts that individuals adopt particular behaviours in response to their labels and that others' perceptions of these actions help to reinforce the original label. (Ibid.: 374–6)

It is important to bear these perspectives on labelling in mind as we turn our attention to 'higher-ability learners'.

Higher-ability learners

There are many ways of referring to 'higher-ability learners', with different terms having endured varying degrees of popularity and dominance within the educational landscape. Typically, these usually involve one of the following words or phrases: able, more able, higher ability, gifted, talented, high achievers, etc. For ease, we will use the term 'higher-ability learner' throughout this chapter in order to indicate a learner whose abilities and therefore potential achievements are significantly above average.

When we move from the term itself to a working definition of a 'higher - ability learner', things get even more complicated. Hymer and Michel explain that it is difficult 'to move beyond a recognition of existing high-level performances and to work towards the demonstration of high achievement in its many forms for all its students' (2002: 9) when constructing a definition of 'higher-ability learners'.

For many teachers, definitions of 'higher-ability learners' in school will be rooted in student performance. In 2016, the UK government's Chief Inspector of Schools in England, Michael Wilshaw, published a commentary on the performance of 'most able' learners that was based on a definition of these learners as 'those that reached Level 5 in the specified subject (English and/or Maths) at Key Stage 2. Pupils who achieve a Level 5 at Key Stage 2 are expected to achieve a grade B in that subject at GCSE. Some pupils may go on to achieve a grade A or A*' (Office for Standards in Education (Ofsted), 2016). This definition purely focuses on attainment and is most relevant for secondary schools, with the focus on the expected progression of these 'most able' learners guiding target-setting for GCSE qualifications. As you may have noticed, the references to Key Stage 2 levels and GCSE alphabet grades are out of date as the government has moved to a new curriculum and assessment system. However, the definition highlights the data-driven nature of identification of 'higher-ability learners' in many schools and pays little attention to academic theories of giftedness or high ability. For more information about these theories, see the Further Reading recommendations at the end of this chapter.

The principles of effective differentiation

- Know your students
- Know your curriculum and pedagogical approaches
- Trust yourself.

Know your students

Interpersonal communication is a key way to get to know students' likes, dislikes and interests. Through this kind of investment in a positive but professional relationship with learners, teachers can develop a better understanding of their individual identities, supporting a positive classroom culture and effective differentiation.

Whilst we have already highlighted some of the issues with narrow use of attainment data, teachers do make use of a wide range of formative and summative assessments that can inform their knowledge of a learner's strengths and needs.

Summative assessment

The data that is tracked in schools is usually taken from 'summative assessment', whereby learners are tested in a particular way and their numerical marks are recorded and often used to generate a grade or level that indicates their level of attainment in that particular test. This can be a useful starting point when you begin teaching a new class or when you join a new school and want to familiarise yourself with your new group or groups. Summative assessment is usually referred to as 'assessment of learning', typically being conducted at the end of a sequence of lessons or unit of study in order for the teacher, faculty or school to evaluate the effectiveness of the learning that has taken place.

There are obvious limitations of summative assessment, in that a learner's performance can be affected by a range of issues such as the lack of familiarity with the test format or conditions, the impact of emotions such as nervousness and ill health, amongst others. In this way, summative assessment may not provide a wholly accurate reflection of the learning that has taken place for each individual learner, but it can be a useful indicator that can inform the teacher's planning for the future study of the individual learners involved, and even partially help the teacher to reflect on the effectiveness of their teaching methods in this particular context.

Many schools encourage teachers to conduct analysis of summative assessment data. Often, this analysis follows on from the ways that school progress is assessed nationally, but there are other ways of analysing summative assessment data that can sometimes illuminate aspects of classroom practice; for instance, if a teacher finds that a particular group of learners is significantly underperforming in summative assessments, then they can explore some of the potential reasons behind this and seek to address this underperformance.

However, there is an important warning that must be issued here. Alex Quigley, of the Huntington Research School in York, explains that:

> We should be very wary of sub-group analysis. With small cohorts (pretty much every school has a small cohort when it comes to the study of statistics), then sub-divided into even smaller cohorts, we create false results due to an 'insensitivity to sample size'. Put simply, the smaller the sample, the greater the variation. (2018)

It can often feel as though data reigns supreme in schools. In fact, many critics of the performativity culture that has arguably flourished in education (as a result of the neoliberal structure of wider society) highlight an illogical focus on measurability as a key aspect of this control mechanism (Ball, 2003). Page (2017) identifies that the widespread collection, analysis and evaluation of data in schools has the potential to be exploited when used as a proxy for teacher effectiveness. Through the analysis of data in a particular way, an otherwise successful teacher could be identified as underperforming and subsequent interventions could be implemented in order to tackle this.

From our perspective, as educationalists who are committed to a humane, person-centred education system, we see that there is a usefulness to collecting some forms of data. If I have taught a particular unit of work to my GCSE group and my data analysis reveals that the majority of the class could not apply any learning from the unit in a subsequent test, then it is useful for me to reflect on ways in which I can address this disconnection between the intended learning and the actual learning that has taken place in my classroom. However, there is a danger that, far from being an additional lens through which classroom learning is explored, the use of data can become tyrannical. Imagine working in a school in which after every data-collection point each teacher is tasked with reducing a particular gap within their data or with improving the performance of a particular targeted group. The placing of accountability on the teacher for pockets of data-recorded underperformance that are rooted in wider issues that the teacher may not be able to resolve is clearly a shortcut to establishing a stressful, negative school culture.

In our view, data should be a tool that is at the disposal of the teacher, middle leaders and senior leaders, but it should not dominate the day-to-day decision-making of a school. Quigley's criticism of the validity of school-based data is crucial in understanding that there is no positivist truth in terms of school effectiveness. Schools are complex, multifaceted communities that cannot be meaningfully illuminated or revealed as successful or failing through the collection and analysis of invalid data. Data should be used with pragmatism, understanding of its potential limitations and as one aspect of a wider system of exploration.

Formative assessment

In contrast to summative assessment, 'formative assessment' is often referred to as 'assessment for learning', as opposed to 'assessment of learning', and refers to a range of strategies that the teacher uses in order to ascertain the learner's level of understanding of a particular topic or their proficiency in a particular skill and then make adjustments to their teaching in order to promote the learner's progress. For instance, if a primary school teacher had planned to introduce Year 2 learners to compound sentences, but discovered through formative assessment that none of the Year 2 learners could accurately identify a noun or verb, then it would be beneficial for the teacher to revisit the characteristics of nouns and verbs rather than carry on with a topic that relies on this missing knowledge.

Cauley and McMillan provide a useful summary of how formative assessment can be used:

> Effective teachers use formative assessment during instruction to identify specific student misunderstandings, provide feedback to students to help them correct their errors, and identify and implement instructional correctives. Ongoing formative assessment is conducted primarily through informal observations and oral questions posed to students while content is being taught or reviewed. (2010: 1)

With regard to motivation, Cauley and McMillan (2010) link formative assessment with the types of goals that learners work towards. Effective formative assessment is associated with learners setting 'mastery-goals', where learning is viewed as the ultimate goal and challenges are perceived positively, as opposed to 'performance-goals', where the external judgement of performance is perceived as most important. Cauley and McMillan (ibid.) see formative assessment as promoting the setting of intrinsically motivated mastery-goals rather than extrinsically motivated performance-goals. They outline a number of features of effective formative assessment:

- Providing clear learning targets and models of how these can be achieved
- Providing task-specific feedback on progress towards learning targets
- Attributing learner success to effort rather than ability
- Encouraging learner self-assessment
- Aiding learners in setting achievable goals in order to improve.

(Ibid.: 2–5)

Know your curriculum and pedagogical approaches

Bloom's Taxonomy has been a cornerstone of Western approaches to teacher training for over 50 years. The taxonomy was devised in the 1950s but revised in 2001, and describes the following learning goals:

- Remember
- Understand
- Apply
- Analyse
- Evaluate
- Create

(Krathwohl, 2002: 218)

These learning goals are arranged in order, from those that are easiest to achieve (referred to as 'lower order') to those that are most challenging (referred to as 'higher order'). In recent years, some neo-traditional teachers have criticised the skills-based nature of Bloom's Taxonomy, with it being argued that this leads to factual knowledge being marginalised within the classroom. However, the verbs that underpin the 2001 revision of Bloom's Taxonomy (Anderson and Krathwohl, 2001) are clearly predicated on the importance of knowledge. In fact, each verb could be sensibly followed by the noun 'knowledge', with the highest level of the taxonomy referring to the creation of new knowledge, in the same way that the academic community prizes contribution to knowledge as key to the role of a higher education researcher. From this perspective, it is difficult to see any merit in the argument that skill has been divorced from knowledge within the classroom.

With regard to effective differentiation for our learners, Bloom's Taxonomy provides us with a useful conceptualisation of cognitive levels of difficulty. As teachers, we can then plan lessons and activities that enable our learners to move from the development of lower-order skills to higher-order skills over the course of our teaching. Other useful conceptualisations of cognitive levels of difficulty can be found within examination board mark schemes for national qualifications such as GCSEs and A levels, as well as in National Curriculum documentation, which sequences the focus of learning in state schools over the course of chronological years of schooling. We can use all of these in order to devise a journey for our learners, in which they develop their knowledge, understanding and skills in order to flourish as learners.

The potential correlation between the highest level of Bloom's Taxonomy (create) and the internal locus of motivation that is essential for the achievement of intrinsic motivation brings us neatly back to the motivational potential of well-sequenced, increasingly challenging tasks within the learning environment. This motivation continuum is explored in more detail in Chapter 10, but features the intrinsically motivated, internally regulated learner at its pinnacle. The idea of learners being able to create their own versions of particular educational artefacts or even to devise new artefacts as a result of having remembered key information, understood key concepts, analysed how these concepts work and fit together and of having evaluated their usefulness, positions the learner as a contributor to learning rather than a recipient of learning. This could arguably move the learner's regulation system from external – where the teacher evaluates their knowledge, understanding and skill against pre-existing models of success or effectiveness, to internal – where the learner takes ownership of devising a contribution that is perhaps surprising and effective, thus fulfilling Bruner's (1962) requirements of creativity.

There is also a well-being dimension to effective differentiation. During a flow state, we experience feelings of agency and an altered perception of time (Csikszentmihalyi, 2014). The flow state is also associated with increased concentration on the individual's actions during the present moment, the coming together of action and awareness, a loss of self-consciousness, and the sense that an activity is intrinsically worthwhile, with both the process and product being valued. Csikszentmihalyi outlines the importance of the following conditions for an individual to achieve flow:

- An activity must be accompanied by clear goals.
- There should be a balance between the perceived challenge involved in the task and the individual's perception of their own ability level.

- There should be clear and immediate feedback available through-out the activity so that the individual can adjust their approach accordingly.

(Csikszentmihalyi, 2014: 160)

Csikszentmihalyi's flow theory clearly parallels the importance of personal growth or perceived competence within self-determination theory. It also provides us with the tantalising potential of an education system that pursues flow. Csikszentmihalyi (2014) sees the flow state as a key aspect of well-being. He explains that 'viewed through the experiential lens of flow, *a good life is one that* is *characterized by complete absorption in what one does*' (Nakamura and Csikszenmihalyi, 2014: 239, italics in original). We have already briefly considered, in Chapter 2, the potential implications of flow in supporting teachers over the course of their careers. Here, however, it is clear that the potential of flow to create a state of intrinsic motivation provides significant justification for meaningful, informed and impactful differentiation within the learning environment. High-quality differentiation could be a crucial way of ensuring the balance between perceived challenge and perceived ability that lies at the heart of the flow state. Similarly, the importance of feedback to the flow state also reflects a crucial aspect of the typical classroom learning environment. Furthermore, a learning environment that is associated with regular experiences of flow is likely to be viewed far more positively by learners and teachers alike, with potential implications for the levels of well-being of those individuals within the classroom community, too.

CASE STUDY

In an A level English Literature lesson, a teacher devised a two-hour-long outdoor lesson, focused on developing an understanding of Gothic literary conventions. The lesson was designed to take advantage of an architecturally Gothic building on campus (complete with croaking ravens perched on the chimneys) and to introduce the students to their topic for the next academic year in the summer term, following their AS level examinations. Many teachers find that the weeks following examinations in Year 12 (when these examinations are still sat by students, a less prevalent approach due to recent A level reforms in England) can be viewed negatively by students, who are worn out by the challenge of revision and the pressure of their real examinations and are ready for their summer holiday. As such, the teacher wanted to devise an engaging and memorable way of introducing this topic, which would ward off some of the negativity and passivity that had characterised the students' attitudes following their examinations.

The teacher devised a series of tasks, involving identification of Gothic features in a short story that was read by the teacher to the group whilst they sat in a circle on the lawn in the walled garden beside the Gothic building. The teacher also introduced the learners to some of the local legends relating to the Gothic building and explained how these were also common to many Gothic literary texts. Following this, the learners worked in groups to define a list of Gothic literary features and then linked these to quotations from the three texts that they would study in the following year. Although the learners had no knowledge of the plots of each text, the quotations were chosen so as to exemplify key genre conventions and therefore to enable the learners to subsequently evaluate how far each quotation fulfilled our expectations of a Gothic text. This evaluation was conducted through the use of a continuum line, with particularly Gothic quotations being placed close to the building and those deemed 'less' Gothic placed furthest away.

The lesson took advantage of a double timetable block, meaning that it took place over two hours. On walking back to the main building with an armful of resources, one of the students turned to the teacher and asked whether the class would be meeting after breaktime in the classroom or back at the Gothic building for the next part of the 'double lesson'. They were shocked to be informed that the 'double lesson' was over and that the two hours had passed by so quickly. Such feedback is anecdotal, but highly suggestive of a flow state having been achieved, at least for one learner in the group.

Trust yourself

So far, we have explored some key aspects of the role of the teacher, including differentiation and assessment. We have explored the connections between these concepts and some theories of well-being in order to propose a classroom model that uses pedagogy as a tool for promoting learning, underpinned by the idea that effective learning (exemplified within the concept of the flow state) can, indeed, lead to higher levels of well-being.

Returning to Ryan and Deci's 'basic needs for competence, autonomy, and relatedness' (2000: 74) for psychological well-being, we want to make a key point here about the importance of the role of the teacher. It can feel overwhelming, particularly during the early stages of a teaching career, to confront competing evidence from academic research, personal experience and professional discourse on a regular basis. It is important for teachers to be informed in relation to these many forms of knowledge. However, it is also important for teachers to be empowered rather than disempowered by evidence. Ellis et al. argue that:

> Professionals develop competence and knowledgeability by aligning and realigning themselves to the practices of their various core communities, negotiating their boundaries, to make sense in a particular implementation context. (2017: 256)

From this perspective, the varied and often competing nature of the discourses that surround education can be seen as a crucial aspect of professional identity development as a teacher. Whilst Ellis et al. (2017) explore how these key aspects of professional identity formation are enacted during their innovative 'Literacy Clinic' model (whereby trainee teachers work collaboratively in order to support struggling readers across the cognitive, cultural and social, and personal identity domains), the approach itself could, indeed, be explored through the lens of self-determination theory. The collaborative nature of the approach, with trainee teachers organised into teams supporting an individual child, fulfils the core condition of interconnectedness as the trainees draw on the support and perspectives of others as they strive to achieve their goal of supporting the learner in question. The negotiation of key theories and the discussion of these within team meetings can be seen as developing the trainee teacher's sense of their own competence, as they become more familiar with the discourses surrounding particular theories and with ways of implementing them. Similarly, by planning strategies and supporting the learner one-to-one, the trainee teacher is also afforded a significant degree of autonomy.

In this way, we seek to reassure you that, although navigating competing forms of knowledge can feel overwhelming, it is a crucial aspect of your own development as a teacher and it is important for you to take control of this process and exercise your own autonomy. Rather than feeling confused and uncertain in the face of debate, feel free to experiment with different approaches and to explore your own feelings about these. Above all, trust yourself.

The emotional needs of the learner

Whilst we have already considered differentiation and assessment from a cognitive perspective, we now turn to the emotional needs of a learner in a bid to explore how *all* learners can be effectively supported and motivated.

The pastoral role of the teacher is increasingly foregrounded within Western societies. In England, the Department for Education published an advice document focused on 'Mental Health and Behaviour in Schools', which stated that:

In order to help their pupils succeed, schools have a role to play in supporting them to be resilient and mentally healthy. (2014: 6)

Clearly, the emotional needs of learners are important to a successful education system. However, there are some critics of this approach and it seems pertinent to consider these now in order to engage meaningfully with this emotional dimension of education. In their book *The Dangerous Rise of Therapeutic Education*, Ecclestone and Hayes argue that a pastoral focus in schools has resulted in a move 'from the intellectual to the emotional, from the mind to the body, [which] typifies what we have called the therapeutic turn' (2009: 61). Similarly, Ecclestone and Hayes see this 'therapeutic turn' as having marginalised the role of subject knowledge within education. A key aspect of their criticism relates to their identification of key aspects of psychology implemented in schools being focused on deficiency, and mental ill health being universally applied to all young people. In their brief summary of the potential implications of the rise of positive psychology, which itself provides a response to this arguable focus of deficiency, they warn that:

Happiness, like therapeutic goals for the diminished self, such as getting in touch with your emotional side, building self-esteem and confidence, are the by-products of striving for other things. Once this positive by-product becomes a central focus for a coercive education, the outcome will be much more uncertain. (2009: 135)

Ecclestone and Hayes (2009) do offer some interesting critique of the political roots of some approaches to personalised learning, which can, indeed, be seen as a manifestation of neoliberal values relating to consumer choice and the importance of the individual as opposed to the collective, but overall their fears of a watering down of the curriculum seem, from our experiences working in and with schools across a range of sectors, to be hyperbolic.

Whereas Ecclestone and Hayes see the school 'eliding welfare and educational goals and activities' (ibid.: 2) negatively, we see high-quality learning within an engaging, motivating and empowering learning environment as potentially supporting the well-being of all participants. Csikszentmihalyi's conception of flow, alongside our focus on the principles of self-determination theory and the potential application of these ideas within schools, suggest that the challenge of learning itself can promote well-being, thus the educational focus of schooling does not need to be compromised by an overly dominant focus on pastoral care, nor do learners need to be 'pathologised' and 'diminished' as Eccelestone and Hayes argue. However, there are many young people who need personalised, tailored emotional and pastoral support which they should receive from a variety of individuals and organisations, many of which are based in school. This is a crucial aspect of the role of the schools.

The emotional well-being of any human being is important. It would be, in our view, a great travesty if schools and teachers were to reject their responsibility for this. We feel that the principles outlined in this chapter provide a compelling framework for supporting well-being by striving for high-quality teaching and learning, and we are proud to elide welfare and educational goals as, in our experience, these two domains can, indeed, by interrelated. Alongside this, we advocate the importance of pastoral education within schools and see this as an important way to support learners in achieving self-awareness, personal growth and interconnectedness.

The sociocultural background of the learner

Another crucial aspect of supporting *all* learners is rooted in the relationship between their sociocultural background and the education system. For too long there has been an outright demonisation of the working-class family in order to explain the higher achievement of children from more financially advantaged backgrounds and those from financially disadvantaged backgrounds. Whilst there has been significant academic critique of this deficiency model (Skeggs, 2004; Reay, 2017), recent policy has highlighted the significance of home-learning activities such as reading in explaining the achievement gap. In 2015, Schools Minister Nick Gibb explained that:

> the Government's plan for education is raising education standards for all, and narrowing the achievement gap between disadvantaged students and their peers. At the heart of this is a very simple insight: the importance of reading. (Ibid.: 4)

Gibb's view of reading as a key aspect of narrowing the achievement gap can be seen as deeply reassuring for all of us who believe in the importance of reading for both pleasure and educative purposes. However, implicitly, there is the suggestion here that disadvantaged students do not currently read *enough*: there is a hint that working-class families and communities are seen as deficient, compared to their middle-class counterparts.

Crucially, we believe that sociocultural *difference* should not be seen as sociocultural *deficiency*. The process by which working-class learners can be affected by this deficiency discourse is exemplified compassionately by Thomson in her conception of the 'virtual schoolbag' (2002: 1). Thomson describes how every learner brings a 'virtual schoolbag' to school that consists of their experiences, tools and relationships to date, which are usually rooted in their pre-school family and community contexts. Thomson argues that the contents of some virtual schoolbags are valued more highly than others by educational institutions due to 'the congruence between... schoolbag and the school curriculum, and ... ease in the school setting' (ibid.: 8). For some children, the contents of their schoolbag are relevant and they have an immediate advantage in getting to grips with their new environment. For other children, the contents of their schoolbag are deemed irrelevant and they are immediately disadvantaged. In this way, the proficiencies of some working-class children are not always acknowledged by formal schooling, whilst their deficiencies can be pathologised and subsequently become internalised.

The process of internalisation of disadvantage as deficiency can be seen in the findings of some educational researchers, who report that working-class learners are likely to feel deficient when they make the leap to university (Reay, 2003; Mallman, 2017). Mallman uses the legal term 'inherent vice' to describe how working-class learners are likely to perceive their differences from the dominant, middle-class culture as internal deficiencies. With this bleak picture in mind, it is important for us to consider how an educational model built on engagement, motivation and empowerment can help tackle sociocultural inequality.

Crucially, the different perspectives and experiences of learners need to be valued and explored within the classroom environment. Through getting to know our pupils, we can work from their strengths and interests in order to engage them within the classroom environment in a positive way. This strength-focused approach is a core principle of positive psychology. For learners who come from backgrounds that are arguably disadvantaged or marginalised within wider society, it seems a tall order for schools to be tasked with negating the impact of this and reducing any disparity between children's levels of achievements due to their ethnicity, social class or other aspect of their background. However, our principles provide a potential starting point for a more equitable education system. Whilst Geldard and Geldard see educational environments as following typical power structures, in which 'the student has little power or authority and those teaching the student have considerable power and authority' (2010: 35), our vision for classrooms and schools is one in which the agency, competence and interconnectedness of *all* learners and teachers is prized.

In a recent report, UNICEF places the UK in 25th place for the inequality gap in educational achievement between the 'average child' and 'the poorest children' (UNICEF, 2016: 4), behind countries including Norway, Ireland, the USA, Canada and Finland. Perhaps more disturbing is the gap between the reported life-satisfaction rates of the poorest children and the life-satisfaction rate of a child from the average financial background, for which the UK is ranked in 20th place. If we tentatively accept a vision of the working-class experience as characterised by both educational inequality and well-being inequality, then our framework for a high-quality education system which views well-being and educational achievement as mutually beneficial goals could perhaps go some way to addressing these gaps.

The wider context of educational inequality and socially just forms of education is too vast to cover here, but we hope that we have provided food for thought in terms of how key well-being principles could be used as a starting point for a socially just model of education. The next steps are yours: in your practices, in your classroom, in your school, you can implement, adapt and evaluate the usefulness of these principles in motivating *all* pupils. You can make a commitment to engage, motivate and empower all learners as individuals and members of a classroom community, rejecting an arbitrary approach to differentiation and instead embracing a principled, humanistic approach.

Chapter summary

- The concept of differentiation is challenged by some neo-traditional teachers in England. We argue that high-quality teaching, effective differentiation and positive classroom relationships support positive behaviours in learners, and that differentiation and inclusion are key aspects of a teacher's role.
- Learners are individuals and their 'ability' level is socially constructed within the school context (Slee, 2014).
- Whilst some degree of labelling allows us to characterise learner experiences and needs, this can be deeply damaging when learners are exposed to these labels or if teachers only view learners through these narrow lenses. Learners are individuals and should be valued as such.
- 'Higher-ability' learners are one example of a 'targeted group' that is often viewed as homogeneous, potentially devaluing the individual learner.
- Our three principles for effective differentiation for *all* pupils are:
  - know your students
  - know your curriculum and pedagogical approaches
  - trust yourself.
- Teachers can make use of a wide range of information in order to get to know their pupils:

- o interpersonal communication
- o summative assessment data
- o formative assessment data.
- In terms of knowing the curriculum and pedagogical approaches, the revised version of Bloom's Taxonomy by Anderson and Krathwohl (2001) provides us with a conceptualisation of the difficulty level of various skills that can be helpful for differentiating in the classroom.
- The careful balance of a learner's ability level with the level of challenge of a task mirrors the conditions required for Csikszentmihalyi's (2014) flow state.
- There are also emotional and sociocultural dimensions to differentiation that can be explored in further detail.

Further reading

Csikszentmihalyi, M. (2014) 'Learning, "flow," and happiness', in *Applications of Flow in Human Development and Education: The Collected Works of Mihaly Csikszentmihalyi*. Dordrecht: Springer.
This will be of interest for those seeking more detail on the relationship between flow, learning and well-being.

Miller, A.L. (2012) 'Conceptualizations of creativity: Comparing theories and models of giftedness', *Roeper Review*, 34 (2): 94–103.
This provides an interesting and detailed exploration of different definitions of giftedness.

Bibliography

Anderson, L.W. and Krathwohl, D.R. (eds) (2001) *A Taxonomy for Learning, Teaching, and Assessing: A Revision of Bloom's Taxonomy of Educational Objectives*. New York: Longman.
Ball, S. (2003) 'The teacher's soul and the terrors of performativity', *Journal of Education Policy*, 18 (2): 215–28.
Bruner, J. (1962) 'The conditions of creativity', in H. Gruber, G. Terrell and M. Wertheimer (eds), *Contemporary Approaches to Creative Thinking*. New York: Atherton.
Cauley, K.M. and McMillan, J.H. (2010) 'Formative assessment techniques to support student motivation and achievement', *The Clearing House: A Journal of Educational Strategies, Issues and Ideas*, 83 (1): 1–6.
Csikszentmihalyi, M. (2014) 'Learning, flow and happiness', in *Applications of Flow in Human Development and Education: The Collected Works of Mihaly Csikszentmihalyi*. Dordrecht: Springer.
Department for Education (DfE) (2011) *Teachers' Standards: Guidance for School Leaders, School Staff and Governing Bodies*. Available at: http://www.gov.uk/government/uploads/system/uploads/attachment_data/file/665520/Teachers__Standards.pdf (accessed 10 January 2018).

Department for Education (DfE) (2014) *Mental Health and Behaviour in Schools: Departmental Advice for School Staff.* Available at: https://www.gov.uk/government/publications/mental-health-and-behaviour-in-schools-- (accessed on 31 December 2017).

Department for Education (DfE) (2016)) 'Mental health and behaviour in schools: Departmental advice for school staff'. Available from https://www.gov.uk/government/publications/mental-health-and-behaviour-in-schools--2 (accessed 20 December 2017)

Ecclestone, K. and Hayes, D. (2009) *The Dangerous Rise of Therapeutic Education.* Abingdon: Routledge.

Ellis, S., Thomson, J. and Carey, J. (2017) 'Generating data, generating knowledge: Professional identity and the Strathclyde Literacy Clinic', in C. Ng and B. Bartlett (eds), *Improving Reading and Reading Engagement in the 21st Century.* Singapore: Springer.

Geldard, K. and Geldard, D. (2010) 'The influence of childhood experiences', in *Counselling Adolescents: The Proactive Approach for Young People*, 3rd edn. London: Sage.

Gibb, N. (2015) 'Foreword', in *Reading: The Next Steps: Supporting Higher Standards in Schools.* London: Department for Education. Available at: http://www.gov.uk/government/uploads/system/uploads/attachment_data/file/409409/Reading_the_next_steps.pdf (accessed 30 December 2017).

Graham, L.J. (2017) 'Student compliance will not mean "all teachers can teach": A critical analysis of the rationale for "no excuses" discipline', *International Journal of Inclusive Education*: doi.org/10.1080/13603116.2017.1420254.

Hymer, B. and Michel, D. (2002) 'Who is gifted? Issues around models and definitions of giftedness', in B. Hymer and D. Michel, *Gifted and Talented Learners: Creating a Policy for Inclusion.* Abingdon: Routledge.

Krathwohl, D. (2002) 'A Revision of Bloom's Taxonomy: An Overview', *Theory Into Practice*, 41 (4): 212–18.

Mallman, M. (2017) 'The perceived inherent vice of working-class university students', *Sociological Review*, 65 (2): 235–50.

Matthews, M.S., Ritchotte, J.A. and Jolly, J.L. (2014) 'What's wrong with giftedness? Parents' perceptions of the gifted label', *International Studies in Sociology of Education*, 24 (4): 372–93.

Nakamura, J and Csikszentmihalyi, M (2014) 'The Concept of Flow', in *Flow and the Foundations of Positive Psychology: The Collected Works of Mihaly Csikszentmihalyi.* London: Springer.

Office for Standards in Education (Ofsted) (2016) 'HMCI's commentary: Most able pupils'. Available at: http://www.gov.uk/government/speeches/hmcis-monthly-commentary-june-2016 (accessed 30 December 2017).

Page, D. (2017) 'Conceptualising the surveillance of teachers', *British Journal of Sociology of Education*, 38 (7): 991–1006.

Quigley, A. (2018) 'Why can't boys be . . . well, more like girls?', Blog, Research Schools Network. Available at: https://huntington.researchschool.org.uk/2018/01/17/why-cant-boys-be-well-more-like-girls/ (accessed 21 February 2018).

Quinn, D. (2017) 'Longitudinal and contextual associations between teacher–student relationships and student engagement: A systematic review', *Review of Educational Research*, 87 (2): 345–87.

Reay, D. (2003) 'A risky business? Mature working-class women students and access to higher education', *Gender and Education*, 15 (3): 301–17.

Reay, D (2017) *Miseducation: Inequality, education and the working classes*. Bristol: Policy Press.

Ryan, R.M. and Deci, E.L. (2000) 'Self-determination theory and the facilitation of intrinsic motivation, social development, and well-being', *American Psychologist*, 55 (1): 68–78.

Skeggs, B (2004) *Class, self, culture*. London: Routledge.

Slee, R. (2014) 'Evolving theories of student disengagement: A new job for Durkheim's children?', *Oxford Review of Education*, 40 (4): 446–65.

Thomson, P. (2002) 'Vicky and Thanh', in P. Thomson, *Schooling the Rustbelt Kids: Making the Difference in Changing Times*. Crow's Nest, NSW: Allen & Unwin.

United Nations Children's Fund (UNICEF) (2016) 'Fairness for children: A league table of inequality in child well-being in rich countries', *Innocenti Report Card*, No. 13. Florence: UNICEF Office of Research, Innocenti.

8
MOTIVATING TEACHERS

Current context: Initial training and CPD for early career teachers

Darling-Hammond (2017) explains that teachers have undergone a very difficult time in both the USA and England. However, a 'strong professional ideal' is critical if all learners (teachers, trainee teachers and pupils) are to do well:

> While reporters and analysts describe a wave of teacher bashing in the United States . . ., and a 'war on teachers' in England . . . nations that have a strong professional ideal for teaching deliberately celebrate teachers and treat teaching as an important profession with a knowledge base that must be mastered if students are to have equitable opportunities to learn. (Ibid.: 292)

She goes on to contrast the Anglo-Saxon approach to teacher education with that in Finland and Singapore. The latter have highly valued teachers and school leaders, who are the products of a high-quality academic and professional education. In Finland, teaching is second only in popularity to medicine as a profession. Darling-Hammond (2017) argues that it is the long period of training leading to a Master's level of teacher education, along with a society that highly values education, that has led to the current educational success in Finland. It could be argued that the culture and history of Finland are strong factors here, potentially as a result of the long history of cultural dominance and threat of Russia over recent decades and centuries. In contrast, Darling-Hammond (ibid.) explains that many voices in the US federal government have challenged the idea that there is a 'knowledge base for teaching' and the role of universities in the preparation of teachers.

The UK government has given far greater weight to the role of schools in leading teacher education in England (DfE, 2010). This includes a greater role for schools in initial teacher education, professional development and school improvement. Schools could apply to be teaching schools to lead on these elements in England, where they demonstrate high levels of effectiveness in both pupil outcomes and in the capacity for leadership and management. There are now over 500 such teaching schools. Teaching schools, through the School Direct programme and school-centred initial teacher training, now supply about half of the new teachers each year in England. Husbands asks 'What are teaching schools for?' (2014: 31). He explains that teaching schools were conceived as being comparable in their nature to 'teaching hospitals'. Teaching hospitals train medical doctors in medical schools of universities with a strong academic programme alongside the professional demands of the medical role. Whilst there have been some notable successes in school-centred teacher education, there are questions over accountability and therefore surrounding the impact and quality of teaching schools per se. There is consensus that the increasing role of schools in teacher education is a good idea. However, anecdotally, most schools would say that their core role is in the education of children and young people and that they do not have the capacity to take over the initial and continuing professional development (CPD) needs of teachers.

Zeichner et al. (2015) echo the view of many in the field of teacher education, on both sides of the Atlantic, when they say that teacher education is in significant turmoil. Taking a lead from the USA, there has been a move in the control of teacher education from universities to schools and other corporate bodies. In the USA, Teach America, with its corporate links and high values in terms of making a difference in schools in challenging circumstances, has become a model for alternative approaches in England. The Teach First model of pre-service training includes a short summer school, followed by trainee placements with high levels of teaching (around

80 per cent of the weekly timetable) from the beginning of the year. Whilst the annual allocation of training numbers to Teach First now runs into the thousands, there is some doubt about the scalability of this approach. It has a sizeable marketing presence in the sector, but evidence of cost-effectiveness, retention and impact on pupil achievement in England is lacking (Allen and Allnutt, 2017).

Zeichner et al. (2015) are clearly mistrustful of the move towards corporate/entrepreneurial models of pre-service teacher education and suggest that this will worsen the quality and opportunities for high-quality teacher education. Looking back at the literature of teacher education in the 1990s, one would have been convinced that we would be looking forward to decades of liberation in teacher education, with teachers taking ever more control of their professional development to liberate learning for the benefit of pupils and teachers. There were great ambitions to create learning communities that would indeed impact on the quality of learning. For instance, Aspinwall (1992) looked forward to a cadre of school leaders who would be able to create professional communities of learning. These, she posited, would provide opportunities for individual and collaborative development. If one thing has changed, it is the greater focus on learner outcomes in pupils in more recent approaches to developing staff (Richey and Nokes-Malach, 2013). Richey and Nokes-Malach (ibid.) focus on the balance of support and challenge from the teacher and expectations of resilience from the learner. Wood and Anderson (2003) highlight the need for a more differentiated examination of the professional learner, recognising that not all teachers have the same motivation, for instance in the early part of their career compared to later. Differentiated learning is clearly as important for teacher education as it is for younger learners. This chapter will examine the motivation of teachers and the different approaches to professional learning. These will be linked to different models of professional development and leadership.

REFLECTION POINT

Your story as a teacher

Use the following questions to help you reflect on your own journey in becoming a teacher:

1. How did you/will you train as a teacher?
2. Was/is this through a school-based programme?
3. What is the role of a university in your training?

(Continued)

(Continued)

4. Do you believe that teachers are trained or educated?
5. What is the role of school experience in developing teachers?
6. What is the role of theory and evidence-based practice in teacher education?
7. How has this impacted on your role as a teacher?

Your reflection will help you to make explicit some of your own beliefs about teacher education and professional development.

Different models of CPD and professional development for trainees and early career teachers

The title of Scales et al.'s (2018) article is poignant: 'Are we preparing or training teachers?' Of course, there is a continuum of practice in professional development in schools, just as there are different motivations for joining the profession. But it is worth analysing the expectations and roles of the teacher in a learning organisation. Figure 8.1 identifies factors that we believe lead to a good education. This is a mastery of learning: cognitive, social, emotional and ethical dimensions across a wide range of domains. We believe that a good education is founded on an agency- and principle-based approach in schools – for both pupil learners and teacher learners. These are explained below, first with reference to a model of agency and principle in teacher education.

In Figure 8.1, teaching and learning agency is the control effected by learners and teachers in a school setting. This relates to the manner in which a pupil learns and the choices they make in that learning journey. Likewise, teachers can be fully active leaders of learning or they can be followers of a teaching system without understanding. In less agentive teaching, learning becomes an act of compliance, as does the role of the teacher. Principle-based teaching and learning is based on a clear understanding of learning, underpinned by knowledge of explicit educational principles and an evidence base to corroborate the approach to teaching and learning being employed by the school and teacher. We stipulate that knowledge alone does not constitute principle-based learning – a strong ethical dimension based on appropriate values is also essential. Of course, there are examples of school curricula and teaching based on a system with little justification. By implication, we suggest that with a lack of learning

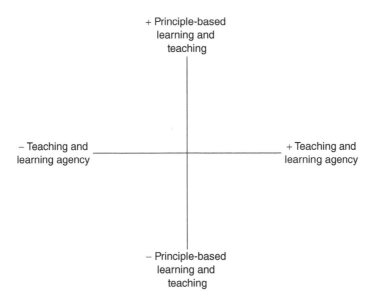

Figure 8.1 A model of good education: Learning agency and principle-based learning and teaching

agency and without a principle-based approach to teaching and learning, a good education is unlikely for both pupils and teachers. We would not want to caricature schools as being Dickensian factories of learning – but most educationalists would recognise that some schools and networks of schools espouse more or less agency in teachers and learners and a principle-based approach to learning and teaching. To be even more accurate, if we were able to draw a third dimension to Figure 8.1, we would add short- to longer-term impact. It is clear that short-term gains in superficial learning can be made through a didactic system's approach to learning, in which learners are led through a mechanical programme; but we would question the longer-term impact – how much learning is retained and what kind of learning is valued.

For teachers, 'agency' and 'principle' are just as important. Kostiainen et al. (2018) explained that effective teacher education has to be both pro-fessionally and theoretically meaningful. For instance, a Master's programme may be attractive at the level of theoretical and academic validity, but if it is not closely aligned to the work of the teacher, then they are unlikely to see it as being meaningful. Teachers on such programmes may not see the rel-evance of such studies. Without relevance, why should they engage with the programme? Meaningless teacher education programmes for pre-service as well as qualified teachers are unlikely to develop high-quality teachers.

They will not translate to the classroom. They are unlikely to translate into improved teacher practices and a good education for pupils. Kostiainen et al. (2018) explain that meaningful teacher education involves the interpretation of new information and connecting this with prior knowledge both at a cognitive level and at a professional level. This interactive view of professional development sees the teacher as an active constructor of meaning. The academic and theoretical understanding interacts with the professional experience of the teacher to make a difference in the lives of the learners through the activities of the teacher. Kostiainen et al. (ibid.) call this constructive, active, intentional, relational and authentic. This recalls discussion of the social, relational and autonomous elements of self-determination theory (Deci and Ryan, 2008).

The intentional, relational and authentic elements to Kostiainen et al.'s (2018) analysis are very important since they describe the best teacher education as being a social and professionally situated experience in an authentic school context. This is not particularly new. Professional development in authentic contexts is more meaningful to teachers; it is more engaging and therefore likely to have more chance of changing the underlying practices of the teacher and impacting on class learning. Whilst Kostiainen et al. (ibid.) focus on school and university partnerships for initial teacher education programmes, there is much to learn here for professional development of qualified and experienced teachers. Emotional learning and emotional engagement with the learner seem to be important in teacher education, alongside knowledge of pedagogy and subject didactics. In fact, one could say that discourse with learners, enthusiasm for a subject and professionalism in dealing with students are integral to pedagogy. Teacher education programmes for pre-service and experienced teachers need to build in these elements to ensure a valid experience. Engaged teachers are more likely to engage learners in the classroom. We return to the work of Zeichner et al. (2015) to explain how this should happen.

Zeichner et al. (ibid.) draw on the work of Engeström (2001) to explain the need for a hybrid approach to teacher education that recognises the unique contributions of both university and school in collaboration. Knowledge, critical analysis and authentic experiences are distributed across the university and school system. Engeström's (2001) cultural historical activity provides a framework for explaining the experience of pre-service and early career teachers. Whether training is provided by a university or a school, the novice teacher is participating in activity systems at the university, in their school placement and possibly within the community in which the school is situated. Each of these systems has varying constraints and aids to support novice teacher learning. However, all too often, these systems are not in dialogue and leave the novice teacher as the sole mediator of multiple-knowledge sources (Zeichner et al., 2015). Without support, the teacher will struggle to make sense of the situation. Engeström (2001) suggests four questions in analysing any learning using activity theory:

1. Who are the subjects of learning, how are they defined and located?
2. Why do they learn, what makes them make the effort?
3. What do they learn, what are the contents and outcomes of learning?
4. How do they learn, what are the key actions or processes of learning?

These questions are used below to examine alternative approaches to professional development in school.

CASE STUDY

In a primary school that has focused on 'set' learning for a number of years, there is a growing recognition that classifying children on the basis of specified attainment in English and mathematics, and then teaching them as a homogeneous group, does not recognise the various needs of individuals and their entitlement to a personalised approach to learning.

A personalised approach to learning has been seen to be effective in other partner schools, and a recent school inspection questioned the 'set' approach to learning.

Applying the questions from Engeström (2001) to an MA student employed in school, as a teacher, these are some of the considerations for professional development.

An MA in Education action research project

1. Who are the subjects of learning, how are they defined and located?

The main subject is the teacher researching her own classroom practice and, by implication, the wider practices of the school. She is defined as an employee of the school as well as a student of the university with whom she is registered. She is physically located in the school as a teacher, but at times attends university tutorials and seminars, sometimes virtually (by phone and Skype) and at other times physically. It should not be underestimated that the voices of all of those in the situation are included in the research. So, if the teacher is the main subject of learning, there is also a dialogue with other staff (teaching assistants, teachers), managers, parents and ultimately pupils.

(Continued)

(Continued)

2. Why do they learn, what makes them make the effort?

The teacher is registered on an MA Education programme. There can be at least two ways of examining her motivations: wanting to gain a Master's because of career and professional aspirations; to develop a deeper understanding, in itself, will be potentially engaging and motivating; and there is likely to be a strong sense of wanting to improve her approaches to teaching in order to improve the quality of learning in her pupils. This may be the subject of a school improvement target and therefore part of the performance management demands of the teacher. So, there are both intrinsic and extrinsic motivations for the teacher.

3. What do they learn, what are the contents and outcomes of learning?

The teacher reads about personalised learning, potentially visiting other schools (either virtually or in person) where this has been embedded with success and carries out a small-scale research project to trial a more personalised approach to learning. This project is undertaken with the knowledge and agreement of the head teacher, who already has concerns about the 'set' approach to learning. The small-scale research provides evidence of the pros and cons of personalised learning in a mixed-ability class of 25 pupils. Hard data of pupil progress demonstrates that pupils make at least the same amount of progress as in 'set' classes. This provides a detailed case study of personalised learning, which the teacher disseminates in a staff meeting at the end of the project. The head teacher considers, alongside the senior management team, whether the school should now move from 'set' to personalised learning.

4. How do they learn, what are the key actions or processes of learning?

The academic thesis submitted for the MA in Education is a vehicle for school improvement, alongside the professional and academic aspiration of the teacher. Whilst the dissertation is established with a school enquiry focus, there is only minor interchange between the school and the university. To a certain extent, the university provides a cachet for the validity and quality of research. The process of research design is situated within a clear and detailed ethical and methodological framework. It leads to greater understanding of a professional situation by reference to prior academic and professional knowledge in this area. At a personal level, tutorials with the teacher provide a Socratic dialogue to 'unpick' the understanding of the topic, recognising that knowledge and practices are almost always uncertain and problematic. The teacher, in supervision sessions as well as the written dissertation, provides a justification for the choices made in the account of personalised learning. An advantage of the university supervision is that it provides a 'safe' space outside the school for the learner to explore new ideas, analysing and rejecting or accepting as appropriate.

Figure 8.2 characterises the two settings of university and school in the above case study as two activity systems working side by side.

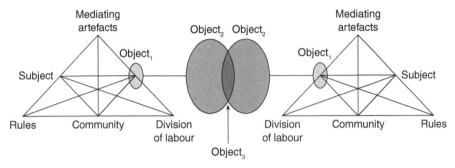

Figure 8.2 Engeström's activity model (2001) reprinted by permission of the publisher, Taylor & Francis Ltd, http://www.tandfonline.com

Whilst the university and the school are, indeed, separate systems, they have some common mediating artefacts (ways of understanding and tools for understanding learning in school), some common rules (like the Teachers' Standards that govern the requirements of teachers and their professional conduct) and intersecting communities (such as teacher mentors for trainee teachers and university visiting tutors for trainee teachers). The common object at the intersection of the two systems is 'personalised learning' and the desire to support change and improvement. In Engeström's (2001: 133) activity theory, it is worth recognising that the two systems have a scaffolding but also a constraining function – there are some things you can do and some things you can't do in the setting. Whereas the university setting might focus on the individual activity of the teacher, the school setting requires a more collegial integration of developments to ensure consistency, scalability and manageability.

Informal professional development for early career teachers

Informal approaches to teacher education located in the third space between universities and schools are developing as a result of a growing frustration with both school and university approaches to professional development. Dreer et al. (2016) explain that more informal approaches to professional development can be motivating for teachers. Lesson study involves small groups of teachers within or even across schools focusing on a particular issue and then collaboratively developing practice through co-planning and peer observation to identify how best to impact on pupil learning. A school-based enquiry can also replicate the type of study identified in the MA research explained in the case study above. In the period from 2010, schools in England have become more interested in carrying out school-based research. The systematic nature of school enquiry is a significant factor in developing high-quality professional development. A 'closed-loop' approach to professional development, in which the same ideas are circulated within a small group of schools, can lead to stale ideas and a lack of innovation. External change agents and practitioners from outside the group of schools can therefore provide a fertile ground for new ideas and school innovation.

Social media provides opportunities to share, search for and disseminate new ideas in teaching through platforms such as Twitter, Facebook, Pinterest, Google, Instagram and LinkedIn. Greenhalgh and Koehler (2016) provide an alternative approach for professional development, using social media. They call this the 'just-in-time' approach to professional development. Although just-in-time professional development is not a formalised concept built on a foundation of empirical evidence, it is a useful metaphor for professional development organised around flexible structures that emerge when necessary and disappear when no longer needed. As opposed to typical approaches, in which facilitators organise the curriculum and use predetermined structures to guide the training and learning, just-in-time professional development is driven by teachers who use flexible structures to find knowledge brokers. The example given by Greenhalgh and Koehler (ibid.) focuses on the use of a Twitter posting in France, following a terrorist attack. The tweet asked how the teacher should respond in school to the attack. This is an interesting conception of professional development. Whilst it probably provides the teacher with some views on how to respond in school to terrorism, it does not overtly seem to provide answers to pedagogical questions. The just-in-time nature of such professional development could result in some ill-considered ideas of a superficial nature that are not thought through in their application to the teacher's own school. On the other hand, it is quite feasible that Twitter responses can signpost teachers to other resources that have already been produced. This is a good example of 'knowledge brokerage' – the use of social media to share information rather than to create new information. There are other anecdotal examples of teachers wanting to plan lessons around certain topics. Tweeting questions can provide a range of useful responses for lessons, but is this professional development?

The above discussion of social media for professional development suggests a continuum from deeper to more superficial teacher learning. We believe that social media can provide teachers with opportunities to engage with principle-based approaches to teaching and learning. Whether one message of 280 characters can, in itself, lead to change is debateable. However, it is quite possible in the interconnections that social media provides, that this one message can signpost the teacher to a greater range of resources.

According to Kostiainen et al.'s (2018) model of meaningful teacher education, the connected space of social media provides relational, agentive and authentic opportunities for teachers to share approaches to teaching. Blended versions of this can be seen in the concept of the Teach Meet (@RossMcGill, 2014). Often associated with existing networks or meetings, this focuses on short presentations by teachers on subjects of common interest. These can be very engaging presentations, with lots of interest from teachers in after-school and weekend sessions. Again, the depth of information provided is questionable, but it does provide teachers with opportunities to explore different approaches to teaching in a quick and engaging way.

The moral of this is that social media and Teach Meets provide an opportunity to engage with different ideas as a starting point, but that greater depth of professional engagement is needed in order to sustain long-term change for the better. The motivational aspect of social media and Teach Meets, on the other hand, does provide a model for layered approaches to professional development. In professional development and teacher education, one size does not fit all.

Characteristics of motivating schools

No one who works in education underestimates the role of motivation in the individual teacher and school (Alexander, 2008) in securing a good education for children. As Alexander (ibid.) states, there are challenges in teaching. These come from outside the teacher (other colleagues, management, children, parents, and on a macro-level, government-inspired changes to the life of schools) and inside the teacher. Internal challenges can be more debilitating – for example, a loss of confidence and long-term mental health difficulties – along with frustration rising from conflicting values. Likewise, different individuals are attracted to the teaching profession, and they all experience differing levels of challenges and satisfaction in their professional lives. Following Alexander (ibid.), we could posit the same profile of challenges for school pupils of internal and external challenging, and of individual learners experiencing different degrees of success and challenge. Furthermore, school leaders could be seen in the same light. Here we have a common set of characteristics: internal and external challenges that are differentially experienced by individuals, leading to differing degrees of success. We are here particularly concerned with early career teachers.

The transition from pre-service training to becoming a fully fledged teacher is the subject of much consideration in the academic literature around teacher education (Alexander, 2008; Malmberg, 2008; Scales et al., 2018). Alexander (2008) focuses on the degree of intrinsic motivation in new teachers just entering the profession. She suggests that many come into the profession with high ideals and the desire to 'make a difference'. However, following qualification and on appointment as a member of staff, such altruism dissipates, to be replaced by a greater sense of realism, whilst it is acknowledged that as many as 30 per cent of teachers leave the profession in England within five years of qualification. Is it the dissipation of hope, and altruism, along with a growing sense of realism that leads professionals to leave? According to Kieschke and Schaarschmidt (2008), teachers develop coping strategies to prevent burnout, which equip them with ways of dealing with the internal and external challenges in school. One such approach is 'emotional distancing' (ibid.). Alexander (2008) challenges this notion on the grounds that being an 'emotionally closed' teacher is not necessarily what is needed in school. Learning how to be emotionally open but not emotionally fragile is an important balance to be achieved. Motivation is a characteristic of teachers as they navigate the internal and external challenges in school.

Deci and Ryan (2008) provide a framework for analysing motivation in teachers. In the move from trainee teacher, we can see a move in the various degrees and dimensions of self-determination:

Connected: Trainee teachers often move from an identity as a student who is a teacher to a teacher who was a student. They may retain a loyalty to their original training institution. This might lead to completion of an MA in Education. However, the professional community as a student will necessarily change as the new teacher enters the professional community of the school. They will relate to new colleagues, children and parents in a changing social and professional world.

Autonomous: Trainee teachers do not always have the opportunity to make curriculum and pedagogical decisions of a long-term nature in school. They can choose aspects of lesson planning and how activities are delivered but, depending on the placement, this can be limited. As qualified teachers, autonomy might still be constrained but for different reasons.

Growing: Individual trainee teachers may grow at different rates. The process of developing, consolidating and extending their professional expertise will probably extend over the continuum of initial training to several years into their career as teacher. What is interesting here is to consider what growth means to an early career teacher. Of course, the professional expertise is important, but personal growth, financial stability and the emotional journey of becoming an effective teacher, all provide opportunities to develop motivation for teaching in school. (Deci and Ryan, 2008: 15)

Of course, there are different models of initial teacher education, with different opportunities to be employed as a trainee teacher. But all have the trainee teacher as part of a wider cohort learning to become teachers. Whilst a contract date for a newly qualified teacher might give the illusion of a clear door through which the new teacher passes, Alexander (2008) along with many others would see the transition to becoming a teacher as being more of a continuum. In England, this is called an 'induction period'. Historically, this also used to be a period of probation for newly qualified teachers. 'Induction' and 'probation' are usually concurrent processes; however, there is a significant difference between the two. Assessment for probation is carried out to determine professional proficiency and to ensure that the individual is able to meet the minimum requirements of the job. Induction is the starting point for learning about the new school and for long-term professional development. There would appear to be a period of de facto probation for new teachers, following assessment by managers in the school in which a new teacher is employed. It is in the new teacher's interest to ensure that they are meeting the expectations of a teacher as interpreted in the school in which they are employed. This analysis could explain the move towards a position of realism rather than idealism in the new teacher. Whether we like it or not, some practices in the employing school will be non-negotiable. A teacher must comply with these expectations, therefore, if they want to continue as a qualified teacher. The degree of space and support a school provides for the new teacher is likely to provide different motivational opportunities, from 'You're in my school now and you do as I say' to 'I will help you to grow as a professional and to forge your own style of teaching'. Of course, most schools will provide a combination of motivations: 'I want you to grow as much as possible as a professional, within the confines of this school, for the benefit of the children.'

REFLECTION POINT

Wood and Anderson (2003) identify characteristics of successful continuing professional development in schools:

- **New entrants and experienced practitioners:** Managers should segment their workforce to identify the needs of particular groups (by gender, age, experience and responsibility).
- **Time and resources:** Whilst time and resources are always a consideration for staff, professional development is too important to be contingent

(Continued)

(Continued)

on funding streams that ebb and flow. Once the benefits in teaching and learning are recognised, concerns about the time to carry out professional development tend to dissipate.

- **Networks and relationships:** Are as important as the structures and processes put in place for professional development.
- **Open culture:** Leads to a spirit of continual improvement, being open to new ideas, and particularly open to the voice of pupils.

Consider your school in relation to the above characteristics. How far does your school include these dimensions for professional development?

There is bound to be a continuum of practice in each dimension, but what can you do as a practitioner in your own practice to change the professional development ethos of the school?

Professional development can sometimes focus on the knowledge aspects of teaching, whereas social, emotional and moral issues are at the root of a teacher's motivation. Bullough and Hall-Kenyon (2011) highlight this in their analysis of the call to teach and teacher hopefulness. By the 'call to teach' we mean seeing teaching as a vocation rather than just a job. These teachers find intrinsic motivation in their roles. They tend to have a strong sense of self-efficacy, work harder and want to keep learning. Teacher hopefulness encapsulates 'academic optimism' and is associated with teachers who are better at problem-focused coping and display greater agency in the light of negative feedback. Bullough and Hall-Kenyon (ibid.) explain that not all experience is educative; in fact some is 'miseducative'. For this reason, more experienced and effective teachers placed considerable investment in their own learning and growth. Maintaining and deepening teachers' investment and commitment to teaching are crucially important to improved practice and are therefore central to the importance of any successful effort at school improvement.

Duke (2014) demonstrates that university leadership programmes for senior leaders can lead to significant improvement in low-performing schools. The role of professional development for early career teaching in low-performing schools is also particularly relevant, since many newly qualified teachers find their first jobs in less-popular, low-performing schools. The knowledge and skills needed by senior leaders of such schools is therefore equally relevant for early career teachers:

- Awareness of the problems that must be addressed and the obstacles that must be overcome in order to raise performance.

- Understanding why the problems and obstacles exist.
- Planning that provides the focus and direction necessary to guide action and maximise impact.
- Competence to address the problems and overcoming the obstacles.
- Commitment to address problems and overcoming obstacles.

Effective professional development should be led by experienced leaders, who have demonstrated that they can support low-performing schools to improvement, delivering authentic programmes. They should offer coaching and continuous feedback as the teacher learners apply their new skills in their own schools (Duke, 2014).

To end this chapter, we return to the central question posed by Scales et al. (2018). Is teacher education preparation or training of teachers? Scales et al. (ibid.) firmly espouse the role of 'teacher judgement' that goes beyond system-learning, to recognise a principled approach to children's and teachers' learning. Using professional judgement is critical for teachers because they constantly make instructional decisions to meet learning needs. Therefore, professional judgement should be prioritised in initial teacher education. How candidates change and grow in their use of professional judgement to make instructional decisions should be clarified. Supporting teachers to reflect on and adapt instruction will help them to develop better learning in their own students.

Learning to teach literacy, for instance, is not simply learning content, skills and strategies, but is a way to think about teaching as a flexible, adaptive process that takes into account the school culture, teacher expertise, curricular demands and student needs. Teachers need to make professional judgements during teaching, and perhaps even become subversive in adaptations, depending on their teaching contexts. They will sometimes need to say 'No' when they are asked to do something that goes against their professional instincts. Indeed, we are not advocates of replicating curriculum instructors or a 'clone army' of teachers who compliantly do as they are told. Instead, teacher education needs to tap into unique sets of skills, experiences and beliefs that teachers bring to a programme of professional development (Scales et al., 2018).

Chapter summary

- Finland and Singapore have highly valued teachers and school leaders, who are the products of a high-quality academic and professional education.
- The UK government have given far greater weight to the role of schools in leading teacher education in England (DfE, 2010). This includes a

greater role for schools in initial teacher education, professional development and school improvement.

- A good education is founded on an agency– and principle-based approach in schools – for both pupil learners and teacher learners.
- There is a need for a hybrid approach to teacher education that recognises the unique contributions of both university and school, in collaboration. Knowledge, critical analysis and authentic experiences are distributed across the university and school system.
- In Engeström's (2001) activity theory, it is worth recognising that the two systems have a scaffolding but also a constraining function – there are some things you can do and some things you can't do in the setting.
- A 'closed-loop' approach to professional development, in which the same ideas are circulated within a small group of schools, can lead to stale ideas and a lack of innovation. External change agents and practitioners from outside the group of schools can therefore provide fertile ground for new ideas and school innovation.
- As Alexander (2008) states, there are challenges in teaching. These come from outside the teacher (other colleagues, management, children and parents, and on a macro-level, government-inspired changes to the life of schools) and inside the teacher. Internal challenges can be more debilitating: for example, a loss of confidence and long-term mental health difficulties, along with frustration rising from conflicting values.
- Bullough and Hall-Kenyon (2011) highlight this in their analysis of the call to teach and teacher hopefulness. By the 'call to teach', we mean seeing teaching as a vocation rather than just a job. These teachers find intrinsic motivation in their roles. They tend to have a strong sense of self-efficacy, work harder and want to keep learning. Teacher hopefulness encapsulates 'academic optimism' and is associated with teachers who are better at problem-focused coping and display greater agency in the light of negative feedback.
- Scales et al. (2018) firmly espouse the role of 'teacher judgement' that goes beyond system-learning to recognise a principled approach to children's and teachers' learning. Using professional judgement is critical for teachers because they constantly make instructional decisions to meet learning needs.

Further reading

Kohli, R, Picower, B., Martinez, A. and Ortiz, N. (2015) 'Critical professional development: Centering the social justice needs of teachers', *International Journal of Critical Pedagogy*, 6 (2): 7–24.

The authors explain the importance of values and the ethical aspect of teaching. Teaching is neither a science nor an art, but a vocation based in social justice, from this perspective.

Alexander, P.A. (2008) 'Charting the course for the teaching profession: The energizing and sustaining role of motivational forces', *Learning and Instruction*, 18 (5): 483–91.
This article explains the factors that sustain teachers in their work, with a particular focus on motivation, both internal and external to the teacher.

Zeichner, K., Payne, K.A. and Brayko, K. (2015) 'Democratizing teacher education', *Journal of Teacher Education*, 66 (2): 122–35.
The author is a towering figure in American teacher education. He focuses on the teacher and why some recent entrepreneurial and commercial aspects of teacher education are unsatisfactory.

Bibliography

@RossMcGill (2014) *Bridging the Gap between Academic Research and Classroom Practice*, @SLTeachMeet, Special Edition, Te@cherToolkit. Available at: http://www.teachertoolkit.co.uk/2014/07/17/bridging-the-gap-between-academic-research-and-classroom-practice-by-slteachmeet/ (accessed 31 December 2017).

Alexander, P.A. (2008) 'Charting the course for the teaching profession: The energizing and sustaining role of motivational forces', *Learning and Instruction*, 18 (5): 483–91.

Allen, R. and Allnutt, J. (2017) 'The impact of Teach First on pupil attainment at age 16', *British Educational Research Journal*, 43 (4): 627–46.

Aspinwall, K. (1992) *Managing Evaluation in Education: A Developmental Approach*. London and New York: Routledge.

Bullough, R.V. and Hall-Kenyon, K.M. (2011) 'The call to teach and teacher hopefulness', *Teacher Development*, 15 (2): 127–40.

Darling-Hammond, L. (2017) 'Teacher education around the world: What can we learn from international practice?', *European Journal of Teacher Education*, 40 (3): 291–309.

Deci, E.L. and Ryan, R.M. (2008) 'Facilitating optimal motivation and psychological well-being across life's domains', *Canadian Psychology*, 49 (1): 14–23.

Department for Education (DfE) (2010) *The Case for Change: The Importance of Teaching*. London: DfE.

Dreer, B., Dietrich, J. and Kracke, B. (2016) 'From in-service teacher development to school improvement: Factors of learning transfer in teacher education', *Teacher Development*, 21 (2): 208–24.

Duke, D.L. (2014) 'A bold approach to developing leaders for low-performing schools', *Management in Education*, 28 (3): 80–5.

Engeström, Y. (2001) 'Expansive learning at work: Toward an activity theoretical reconceptualization', *Journal of Education and Work*, 14 (1): 133–56.

Greenhalgh, S.P. and Koehler, M.J. (2016) '28 days later: Twitter hashtags as "just in time" teacher professional development', *TechTrends*, 61 (3): 273–81.

Husbands, C. (2014) 'What are teaching schools for?', *Management in Education*, 29 (1): 31–4.

Kieschke, U. and Schaarschmidt, U. (2008) 'Professional commitment and health among teachers in Germany: A typological approach', *Learning and Instruction*, 18 (5): 429–37.

Kostiainen, E. et al. (2018) 'Meaningful learning in teacher education', *Teaching and Teacher Education*, 71: 66–77.

Malmberg, L.-E. (2008) 'Student teachers' achievement goal orientations during teacher studies: Antecedents, correlates and outcomes', *Learning and Instruction*, 18 (5): 438–52.

Richey, J.E. and Nokes-Malach, T.J. (2013) 'How much is too much? Learning and motivation effects of adding instructional explanations to worked examples', *Learning and Instruction*, 25: 104–24.

Scales, R.D.W. et al. (2018) 'Are we preparing or training teachers? Developing professional judgment in and beyond teacher preparation programs', *Journal of Teacher Education*, 16 (1): 7–21.

Wood, D.E. and Anderson, J. (2003) 'Towards the learning profession: Identifying characteristics of successful continuing professional development in schools', *Management in Education*, 17 (4): 21–4.

Zeichner, K., Payne, K.A. and Brayko, K. (2015) 'Democratizing teacher education', *Journal of Teacher Education*, 66 (2): 122–35.

9

ACTIVE LEARNING

Chapter guide

In this chapter, you will learn about:

- Key concepts at the heart of active learning
- Active learning and cognitive psychology
- Key strategies and how to implement them in your practice

If we are to engage, motivate and empower learners, then it is crucial for their learning experiences to be active rather than passive, with learners constructing meaning for themselves. As Swiderski argues, 'most high school teachers . . . embrace the notion of learning as an opportunity for students to work with information in some manner that makes the information meaningful. Indeed, these teachers recognize that learning requires students to be actively involved' (2011: 239).

Active learning can be difficult to define as the approach is implemented in many different ways. Thomas explains that 'the bottom line in active learning is, in order to learn, students must do more than simply listen. With an active learning approach, teachers design instruction that invites students to take action and to reflect on the skills and/or the knowledge required to complete a task' (2009: 13). Here, Thomas implicitly identifies a contrast between learners as active or passive. These two states of being for learners are identified as part of a range of continua by Hilary McQueen (2014) in her book *Roles, Rights, and Responsibilities in UK Education*. McQueen presents 'multiple dichotomies', which can influence the role of the learner within the classroom and, on a wider level, an educational institution as a whole. Within these dichotomies, McQueen highlights the 'active-passive' continuum and defines passive learners as those 'who have less involvement than teachers expect and thus experience educational processes as acting upon them rather than something they contribute to actively' (ibid.: 53). Thomas (2009) sees active learning as 'student-centred' in contrast to 'teacher-centred' approaches such as lectures and direct instruction, which position the learner as a passive recipient of the teacher's knowledge.

Active learning and cognitive psychology

In order to explore active learning practically within our classroom practice, it is important to understand the theoretical background of the approach. Swiderski (2011) situates active learning within two different branches of educational psychology. First, she explains how psychological constructivists assert that 'knowledge consists of mental structures that are built and rebuilt as individuals interact with their environment. Each structure is an organized body of information that is amenable to change when an individual encounters a new idea' (ibid.: 240). Swiderski outlines two key concepts within this approach:

- 'Assimilation' refers to the process of 'enlarging an existing structure to allow for the inclusion of a new idea'.
- 'Accommodation' refers to the process of 'making an existing structure more complex or creating a new structure.' (Ibid.: 240)

From this perspective, the involvement of learners in active learning enables them to assimilate or accommodate ideas in the context of their pre-existing knowledge and thus build on or adapt what they already know.

Second, Swiderski explains that active learning can be seen as rooted in the work of information processing theorists. Information-processing theorists argue that memory consists of three components:

- The 'sensory memory' is 'engaged when information from the environment is encountered and perceived' (ibid.).
- 'Working memory' is 'used when the information from the "sensory memory" is temporarily stored and processed, or worked with' (ibid.).
- The 'long-term' memory is then used to store knowledge that has already been 'organized into meaningful structured as well as stored in a manner that highlights connections to other structures focused on similar topics' (ibid.). The long-term memory and the working memory can interact in order for the learner to use prior knowledge in order to make initial assumptions or hypotheses relating to new information that is encountered.

Swiderski sees these two branches of educational psychology as providing a theoretical background to active learning, and argues that:

> learning involves not only the building and rebuilding of mental structures as an individual interacts with the environment, but also the representation and storage of these structures in an individual's mind such that, when needed, information can be easily retrieved. (Ibid.)

Topic interest and situational interest

As a teaching approach, active learning is linked to two key concepts related to theories of motivation: topic or individual interest, and situational interest. 'Topic interest' can be defined as 'a manifestation of individual interest defined as a deep personal interest in a field or activity based on pre-existing knowledge, personal experiences, and emotions' (Flowerday and Shell, 2015: 135). For a teacher, then, topic interest is when a learner or learners feel enthusiasm for studying a particular topic, regardless of the manner in which they study the topic. The personal and individual nature of this interest, however, means that it is unlikely to be reflected in an entire class of learners. Similarly, although many learners will experience topic interest, it is unlikely that learners will experience this when learning about every topic within a particular curriculum.

'Situational interest', on the other hand, 'appears to arise from novelty, curiosity, or salient informational content' (ibid.). Flowerday and Shell outline a potential correlation between situational interest and topic interest when they describe how the former 'may be instrumental in catching attention . . . and may precede and facilitate the development of individual interest, which, in turn, serves to hold or maintain interest' (ibid.). Whilst a teacher cannot initially predetermine the individual interest levels of learners in their classroom, through arousing situational interest the teacher could potentially encourage learners to develop individual interest in particular topics they have taught.

Renniger and Hidi agree, in principle, with this idea of a continuum between topic interest and situational interest. However, they go further and actually propose a model of interest development, which features the following four phases:

1. *Triggered situational interest*: This is the phase in which 'people's feelings about their own interest may be positive or negative and may or

may not result in sustained engagement. Triggers in this phase are more likely but not necessarily external to the individual' (2016: 12).

2. *Maintained situational interest*: This phase occurs when the learner is 'likely to continue to develop their knowledge of and value for the content of interest. However, much of the support for the continued development and deepening of interest still comes from features of the environment, including other people, activities and resources' (ibid.: 14).

3. *Emerging individual interest*: This is the third phase of the model and occurs 'when people begin taking initiative by independently reflecting and reengaging, seeking answers and/or identifying resources that allow their knowledge to deepen' (ibid.).

4. *Well-developed individual interest*: This is the final phase and is characterised by learners being 'able to overcome frustrations from needing to rework, or rethink, issues that arise. They are able to recognize others' contributions to the disciplines, may actively seek to understand those contributions, and are likely to seek feedback' (ibid.).

Crucially, for educators, Renniger and Hidi's model has been validated in a number of studies (Lipstein and Renniger, 2007; Nolen, 2007; Harackiewicz et al., 2008), which suggests that this is a useful and reliable framework to explore within the context of both primary and secondary classrooms.

REFLECTION POINT

- Can you think of a point in a lesson when a learner might experience triggered situational interest?
- What kinds of external stimuli could trigger this first phase of interest?
- How could a teacher contribute to the maintenance of this situational interest so that the learner can enter the second phase of interest?
- Are there particular tasks or activities which a teacher could devise in order to encourage a learner to enter the third phase of the model, emerging individual interest?
- Is it possible for a teacher to be able to guide a learner through the fourth and final phase of the model, well-developed individual interest? Why/why not?

Some researchers have seen situational interest as rooted in a lack of knowledge in learners and have therefore concluded that this state can only occur if a learner lacks knowledge about the particular topic in question (Rotgans and Schmidt, 2014). However, it is important to note that in studies where researchers have found that 'increased knowledge diminishes situational interest' (ibid.: 38), it is often unclear as to how they have defined situational interest. The definitions outlined in this chapter draw on the views of Renniger and Hidi (2016) and Markey and Loewenstein (2014) in characterising curiosity and interest as distinct. As such, the relationship between increasing knowledge and decreasing situational interest (which can at first seem troubling) can be explained by creating a clear distinction between situational interest and curiosity. Curiosity 'only results from a desire to close an information gap', whereas interest 'involves engagement in order to learn more about a subject generally' (Renniger and Hidi, 2016: 43). In this way, it becomes clear that it is not *interest* that wanes as knowledge increases, but curiosity.

With regard to active learning, Renniger and Hidi's (2016) four-phase model of interest development clearly places a strong emphasis on the learner as an active participant progressing through distinct phases in order to reach a level of intellectual empowerment that most teachers would be proud of. It is the teacher's role in helping trigger and sustain situational interest to which we turn next.

Triggering situational interest through active learning

Renniger and Hidi summarise a number of ways in which teachers can help to develop interest for their learners:

> An educator's style, instructional technology, and organization of materials may all contribute to learners' interest and performance. For example, they can arrange tasks to actively engage learners, and such enhanced participation is likely to increase students' levels of interest. Teachers can make required content personally meaningful and relevant; they can also include information that is novel, surprising, and complex. Since teachers plan and program curricula, they can improve instruction by sequencing and selecting tasks that enable learners to make and continue to develop their connections to content. Researchers have also reported that human aspects, ethically controversial concepts, suspense, and choice may lead to more sustained student interest. (2016: 129)

Making it personal

At first glance, many assume that making learning personal refers to choosing topics or areas of study with which learners are already familiar or engaged. It is worth defining the term 'personal' here by explaining that we in this context, refer to engaging the learner in meaningful learning experiences on a personal level. This does not necessarily automatically correlate with narrowing the curriculum and a teacher's methods to those with which the learner is already familiar, but rather, gives further context to how situational interest should arise from a personal engagement with a particular learning experience. Through high-quality planning and delivery of active learning experiences, a teacher can inspire and educate a learner regardless of their pre-existing level of topic or individual interest.

Novelty

Novelty is often dismissed as a 'gimmick', yet meaningful novelty is actually a crucial aspect of many definitions of intrinsic motivation and creativity. Having already explored aspects of Deci and Ryan's theory of self-determination in Chapter 6, it is particularly helpful now to assess the value of novelty from this perspective. Although Deci and Ryan see autonomy, competence and interconnectedness as the three key aspects of well-being, they also acknowledge the role of novelty in intrinsic motivation, defining this phenomenon as 'the inherent tendency to seek out novelty and challenges, to extend and exercise one's capacities, to explore, and to learn' (Ryan and Deci, 2000: 70). The idea that novelty is a factor in intrinsic motivation was further explored by González-Cutre et al. (2016). They argue that if individuals seek to practise skills that are novel, then their satisfaction will, accordingly, decrease when these skills are no longer novel. In this way, they seek to distinguish the concept of novelty from motivation, seeing it as a fundamental psychological need in its own right, rather than as an add-on to ideas relating to autonomy, competence and motivation.

Moving from self-determination theory to ideas surrounding creativity allows us to shed further light on the concept of novelty. Cropley and Urban argue that novelty is a 'constant factor in all definitions of creativity' and highlight the importance of novelty in that creativity itself can be seen as the production of ideas that are both novel and effective (2000). If we are to agree that creativity is a valuable skill within the context of an education system, then we would be wise to explore, model and give our learners the opportunity to experience and create novelty. Csikszentmihalyi and Wolfe (2000) emphasise that, whilst novelty is an important aspect of creativity, teachers should not praise novel and divergent ideas merely for the sake of it. They emphasise that learners need to learn to evaluate their ideas and therefore should be encouraged to develop their own criteria of what constitutes a creative, novel and effective idea.

Within the context of education, the teacher may be seen as someone who should enforce the status quo in order to transmit a body of knowledge to individual learners, with imitation being prized over innovation. In contrast, Csikszentmihalyi and Wolfe argue that if 'the curriculum and the methods of instruction will stimulate and sustain students' interests, the likelihood of them being motivated to ask new questions and explore divergent solutions will be enhanced' (ibid.). In this way, the links amongst novelty, creativity, intrinsic motivation and interest become increasingly clear.

Choice

Choice can be linked to Deci and Ryan's self-determination theory, in that it can be seen as providing a way for individuals to exercise their autonomy. However, Ryan and Deci also highlight some of the difficulties associated with the concept of choice:

> One can have many options and not feel autonomy, but instead feel overwhelmed and resentful at the effort entailed in the decision making. Alternatively, one could have only one option (which functionally means no choice) and yet feel quite autonomous so long as one truly endorses that option. Furthermore, choice can, when meaningful, facilitate self-determination, especially when it allows one to find that which one can wholeheartedly endorse. (2006: 1577)

For teachers, this throws up an interesting and pertinent issue with choice in the classroom. Where teachers aim to promote choice arbitrarily, with a vague notion that this will in some way improve their classroom practice, they may, at best, find very little benefit in providing arbitrary choices (perhaps in relation to tasks or reading material) and, at worst, actually cause learners to feel overwhelmed. In this way, whilst providing learners with meaningful choices (in the context of their own learning) can be a powerful way of motivating learners and also empowering them to learn independently in the future, it is important for teachers not to arbitrarily offer choice for the sake of it.

CASE STUDY

In a Year 13 A level English Literature class, the teacher gave learners completely free text choice in order to increase the likelihood of the learners experiencing topic interest (in that they may already be interested in the text or some of its central themes). The teacher also wanted the learners to take more ownership of their coursework as this embraced the independent spirit of the unit as defined by the exam board as well as providing the learners with an important opportunity to exercise more of the autonomy and independence associated with university-level study. Obviously, there was a more intensive degree of effort required from the teacher in that she had to familiarise herself with all the texts the learners proposed and provide advice on the suitability of choices and tasks. However, by giving the learners the opportunity to exercise meaningful choice, engage with advice from a subject specialist and then reflect on the coursework process itself, the learners gained much greater understanding of the process of planning, drafting and editing than if they had been constrained with text choice and tight, arbitrary deadlines.

The teacher had prepared for the independence of the final coursework task by carefully planning, scaffolding and modelling a high-quality approach and outcome previously in her teaching. She decided to use a portfolio approach, teaching a variety of texts and modelling the process of literacy criticism before introducing the final choice for the learners. In this way, the learners did not feel overwhelmed and in fact enjoyed the task more than the other units they had been taught.

We will now explore a number of practical strategies that can be used in order to promote a learner's situational interest in a particular lesson or activity.

Role play and drama in education

Whilst many teachers often dismiss the potential of role play and drama outside of arts and humanities subjects, these strategies provide significant opportunity to encourage situational interest in a learner and also elucidate key study concepts in memorable ways.

A key figure in drama in education is Dorothy Heathcote, who coined the term 'mantle of the expert' in the 1980s to describe a drama approach where 'the teacher assumes a fictional role which places the student in the position of being "the one who knows" or the expert in a particular branch of human knowledge' (Heathcote and Herbert, 1985: 173). Johnson et al.

further elucidate some examples of the 'mantle of the expert' approach by explaining that learners 'might be scientists in a laboratory or archaeologists excavating a tomb, or a rescue team at the scene of a disaster' (2015: 205). They explain that the approach is particularly empowering for learners as it gives them the opportunity to acquire knowledge and skills and then to apply these in lifelike situations.

CASE STUDY

In a joint project between a secondary school and a university education faculty, a group of Year 10 learners who had been identified as 'more able' were invited to conduct a research project focused on the nature of good-quality teaching. The learners held regular meetings in order to make collaborative decisions on how to carry out their research, and designed a questionnaire and organised observations of a number of teachers in their school in order to gain some initial data. The teacher coordinating the project played a facilitating role (e.g., photocopying and disseminating questionnaires, notifying teaching staff of observations, etc.) rather than leading the group, allowing the learners to authentically develop autonomy and independence. The final outcome of the learners' research project was their delivery of a session on the university's PGCE Secondary Programme, which gave them the opportunity to take on 'real-world roles' (Johnson et al., 2015: 203).

The 'mantle of the expert' approach encourages teachers to select a 'dramatic metaphor', 'which involves a group situation and demands interaction with the social system of a given culture' (Heathcote and Herbert, 1985: 174) in order for learners to collaboratively construct their knowledge as they actively participate in the subsequent role play. The options for teachers are vast; however, a selection of ideas are detailed here in order to give a range of examples:

- A history lesson focused on building Year 9 students' understanding of a variety of aspects of the Second World War involved the learners working in groups with a number of historical artefacts and taking on the role of museum curators devising an exhibition aimed at people of their own age. The learners wrote descriptions of the objects and also composed a fictional provenance and scenario to illustrate their possible role in the Second World War for the visitors to the exhibition. Artefacts included a collection of cigarette cards, a soldier's helmet and a pair of vintage field binoculars.

- A Year 10 English Literature lesson focused on consolidating learners' understanding of the key events in a text and developing their ability to use evidence to support an argument and to make and evaluate interpretations of texts in response to a statement. All of these skills are crucial aspects of essay writing. The teacher decided to place a character on trial, with the learners working in groups to take on particular roles within the 'dramatic metaphor' of the court. Instead of the learners using drama to take on the role of particular characters, the teacher wanted them to become involved in the process of establishing facts from the text and then interpreting these for particular purposes. As such, learners who were still struggling with aspects of the text were given the role of the police, using copies of the text in order to establish key events related to the character on trial. Learners who understood key information relating to characters and key events but lacked confidence in their ability to form arguments were given the role of 'forensic experts', analysing the text from a particular perspective and selecting appropriate evidence to justify this view. Learners who were confident in forming interpretations of texts were given the roles of either the prosecution or defence teams, with the latter placing a significant emphasis on the evaluation of interpretations of texts. This opportunity to evaluate is often a key aspect of the highest bands of GCSE English Literature mark schemes and gave the teacher a chance to stretch and challenge some of the most able learners in the classroom at the same time as supporting the knowledge and understanding of other learners.

  Once the groups had collated their evidence and planned their contribution to the whole class activity, the trial began. The prosecution and defence teams used the evidence from the police and forensic experts in order to further support their arguments. Similarly, once the police and forensic experts had delivered their evidence, they assumed the role of the jury and carefully listened to the arguments put forward by both the prosecution and defence teams in order to make their final decision. This format means that all learners are valued for their contribution to the activity, as well as allowing all learners either to practise higher-order skills or to experience high-quality modelling of these.

- In a Year 9 English Literature lesson focused on increasing learners' understanding of the context of Markus Zusak's *The Book Thief* (2005), the teacher allocated different groups of learners different social roles from 1930s Germany and they researched these in order to 'role-play' their attendance at a Nazi rally, with the teacher playing a clip from a television programme in which Robert Carlyle played Adolf Hitler and delivered an English translation of one of the latter's famous speeches. The entire lesson was themed around this, with learners initially participating in a starter activity, in which they analysed a number of propaganda posters that they were told had been on display before the rally, before completing their research task on a worksheet that was themed as an 'event programme'. The opportunity to consider reactions of different social groups to Nazi policies enabled the learners to deepen their understanding of the different reactions of key characters in the novel to the rise of Nazism. It is important to note that the teacher ensured that, although the learners were dealing with a controversial topic, the ideas explored focused on economic and social policies and were not directly linked to the Holocaust. By introducing the learners to an earlier point in the history of German Nazism, the learners made powerful links between these early political policies and the devastating impact that this political ideology had such a short time later, based on their own prior knowledge of the horrors of the Holocaust.

Furthermore, the potential for drama in education approaches is not limited to the subjects previously discussed. Ødegaard puts forward a compelling vision of science education when she describes the following:

> To fulfil its educational potential, science education must seek non-authoritarian and creative learning environments, which enable students to be both critical and curious about science and the world that surrounds them, and at the same time offer them an insight into the value of critical reflections within science and scientific activity itself. (2003: 96)

Braund (2015) builds on Ødegaard's work with a study of the role of drama approaches in teaching learners about human fertilisation. He highlights that the teaching of science at secondary level often relies on concepts and constructs that are very different from a learner's own experiences of the world. Braund argues that drama approaches could 'help these pupils reach a possibly truer and more easily comprehended (more plausible) understanding of an obscured or complex set of truths' (ibid.: 114), exemplifying this with a series of activities linked to the biological processes involved in human fertilisation. He found that the drama approach was particularly effective in highlighting how complex scientific processes can be.

REFLECTION POINT

- Can you think of a particular curriculum topic from your subject or subjects that would lend itself to a drama approach?
- How would your learners potentially benefit from this method of teaching?
- Are there any potential drawbacks to consider?
- How might frequent use of drama approaches affect your classroom culture?

Taking role play further with technology

Lauber (2007) proposes a 'simulations continuum' of learning experiences, which ranges from activities of low sophistication (such as informal discussions and case studies) to those of higher sophistication (such as role plays and other high-fidelity simulations). Here, the opportunities for play and role play through technology are foregrounded, with computer-based simulations providing highly sophisticated, high-fidelity simulations of real-life situations. Quinn summarises the benefits of computer-based simulation:

> in providing practice before any real application . . . we can strip away unnecessary details and focus on underlying abstractions. This can help far transfer. We may alter the timing of important elements so that they come more often than normal to give concentrated practice, or slower than normal to give a chance to learn the necessary skills and gradually acquire the ability to handle them faster. (2007: 143)

If we see role play and drama approaches as relatively sophisticated simulations of learning experiences, then the potential for using recent technological developments in order to provide even more realistic simulations is also interesting. Whilst the development of educational computer games to a professional standard is an incredibly ambitious goal for individual classroom teachers to work towards, the growth of computer-based, 'sandbox' games such as 'Minecraft' have enabled teachers to create computer-based simulations that allow students to role-play and to discover independently within their virtual learning experiences.

Minecraft

Minecraft is one of a number of computer-based games or video games that have been used effectively in the classroom. The game allows the player to interact with a virtual 'world' that features many of the activities familiar to the real world: farming, mining and building. Through using various blocks (made of different materials with different properties) and tools, the player can choose their own objectives and play the game in their own way. The educational potential of this 'sandbox' environment was harnessed through the development of Minecraft Edu, through which teachers can share pre-created 'worlds' with particular themes in order to enable their learners to interact with the game in a slightly more controlled and targeted way.

Nebel et al. (2016) explain that the success of Minecraft has highlighted the following three learning dimensions for computer-based games as learning experiences:

- Learning through playing
- Learning through creating
- Learning through teaching others.

These three dimensions are likely to be very familiar to classroom teachers, highlighting how teachers could explore computer-based games in order to devise simulations that boost learners' levels of situational interest by giving agency and choice, utilising novelty and allowing a personal level of engagement.

CASE STUDY

A Year 3 teacher used Minecraft with his class in order to conduct experiments relating to plant growth virtually. The teacher organised the learners into pairs, with each being allocated a laptop with a pre-installed version of Minecraft Edu. The learners were instructed to conduct their own experiments, focused on how to grow seeds effectively in Minecraft through controlling various conditions. Within Minecraft, various blocks and objects have different properties, for example learners were able to place torches to serve as light sources for their plants or create irrigation ponds to provide water. They were able to exercise their creativity through the virtual experiments, with some building greenhouses made of glass blocks in a bid to speed up

(Continued)

(Continued)

the farming process. As the conditions in Minecraft closely resemble those in real-life farming (on a basic level), the learners were able to create and test hypotheses by manipulating the virtual world. This promoted engagement by reducing the time required for seeds to grow, as well as through the use of the computer-based game format with which the learners are familiar. The teacher was then able to draw on the learners' findings and compare these with the conditions needed for seeds to germinate and plants to grow in real-life situations.

Moving towards independent learning

Whilst the strategies explored so far emphasise the teacher's role in creating a stimulating and engaging classroom environment, there is also a need to support learners in developing their own independence so that they can continue to engage with the world around them in purposeful and meaningful ways after their formal education has ended. Renniger and Hidi see this increasing independence as a key aspect of the development of individual interest, explaining that:

> The shift from adults assuming responsibility for young children's interest development to the children themselves beginning to seek out opportunities and resources is an important step in the development of interest. (2016: 128)

Creativity in learning and teaching

Although we have already touched on some of the links between creativity and novelty in this chapter, showing that an active learning approach can be tied to definitions of creativity in that it encourages the exploration of novelty, we now turn to the potential for harnessing and encouraging creativity through active learning.

Creativity has traditionally been defined as being manifested in those products that evoke surprise but are also effective (Bruner, 1962). From this starting point, various definitions and models of creativity can also be introduced. Csikszentmihalyi and Wolfe (2000) argue that creativity is inherently rooted in social and cultural contexts, in that, in order for a concept or idea to be seen as novel and valuable, it must be viewed in light of what has gone before. Csikszentmihalyi's systems model of creativity helps to bring to light the teacher's role in the development of student creativity, in that it outlines the relationship between:

- The person (e.g., the musician, artist, writer)
- The domain (e.g., music, art, literature)
- The field or 'gatekeepers' (e.g., critics, teachers).

This model highlights that the teacher's role is almost that of a mediator between the learner's ideas and concepts and the domain within which these ideas and concepts fit. Csikszentmihalyi and Wolfe summarise how the systems model can be mapped onto schools:

> If we apply this model to educational institutions, schools might be seen as consisting of the same three components: a body of knowledge to be transmitted (Domain), teachers who controls the knowledge (Field), and finally a number of individuals, the students, whose task is to learn the knowledge and who are evaluated by teachers in terms of their learning. (2000)

The idea of the domain as a body of knowledge that must be transmitted by the teacher does not lend itself to the development of creativity particularly. However, creativity is an important driver of change and is clearly valued within society, suggesting that it must have a greater role in education. This is conceptualised within the model by the idea that the students can vary the knowledge that has been transmitted to them and their teachers can then mediate this into the field itself.

However, Kaufman and Beghetto see this model as focusing on 'Big-C' creativity, or that which represents 'creative greatness' (2009: 1), and instead suggest that there are more everyday forms of creativity that can be explored within the classroom. At the lower end of their 'Four C' creativity model, Kaufman and Beghetto introduced 'mini-c', which 'was designed to encompass the creativity inherent in the learning process' (ibid.: 3). They then describe how a learner can be formally mentored in order to achieve 'Pro-c' creativity or perhaps independently experiment with their creativity within a particular field in order to move into 'little-c' creativity, with informal mentoring predicating the move to 'Pro-c' creativity for learners who have followed this less formal route. Finally, through achieving greatness, a learner can eventually move from 'Pro-c' in order to reach the level of 'Big-C' creativity (ibid.: 7). The use of this model clearly allows teachers to explore ways that 'mini-c' and 'little-c' levels of creativity can be encouraged within their own classrooms, without the pressure of learners being compared with geniuses such as Mozart or Giotto.

Beghetto and Kaufman outline a number of suggestions for developing creativity within the classroom:

- Encourage learners to think creatively by creating their own analogies, analysing problems in different ways and engaging in meaningful evaluation.
- Place an emphasis on student interest, provide some choice in learning activities, allow students independence in solving problems and provide opportunities for collaborative learning.
- Focus on intrinsic rather than extrinsic motivators and root classroom motivation in a positive classroom culture.
- Encourage learners to use creativity and learning in order to achieve other goals, for instance through interesting projects with a real outcome.
- Model creativity by embracing teaching itself as a creative role and endeavour to support the development of key aspects of creativity within the classroom. (2014: 64–5)

We believe that teachers, in implementing the ideas set out in this chapter (making it personal, experimenting with novelty, providing meaningful choice), will be seeking out teaching strategies that are both effective and novel, in this way achieving a level of creativity through their own practice. In turn, by modelling creativity in this way, teachers are honouring some of the principles of creativity in their classrooms and are demonstrating these to learners. Rather than positioning learners as solely passive recipients of knowledge, teachers who embrace active learning are modelling creative practices and enabling learners to help vary transmitted knowledge in new ways through their own 'mini-c' and 'little-c' practices.

Chapter summary

- Active learning is an important way of engaging, motivating and eventually empowering learners.
- There is a dichotomy between active learning and passive learning approaches within the classroom, which is also tied to the dichotomy between teacher-centred and learner-centred approaches.
- The involvement of learners in active learning enables them to assimilate or accommodate ideas in the context of their pre-existing knowledge and thus build on or adapt what they already know.
- Active learning can help to encourage situational interest, which helps to motivate learners in the classroom.

- Renninger and Hidi (2016) propose a four-phase model of interest, which consists of:
  - triggered situational interest
  - maintained situational interest
  - emerging individual interest
  - well-developed individual interest.
- By enabling learners to progress through these phases of interest, the teacher is able to encourage the development of the topic or individual interest (when a learner is already intrinsically interested in the topic being taught or studied).
- Teachers can encourage situational interest by:
  - making learning *personal* for the learner
  - exploring the potential of *novelty* in teaching and learning activities in order to model or promote creativity
  - providing meaningful *choice* for learners in order to encourage them to exercise a degree of autonomy.
- We have also explored the possible dangers or perceived lack of benefit of offering overly numerous or arbitrary choices to learners (e.g., a choice of similar tasks with no distinguishably distinct difference in process or outcome).
- You could use the following practical strategies to embrace active learning in your classroom:
  - role play and drama (e.g., 'mantle of the expert')
  - computer-based games that provide opportunities for virtual role-play and exploration.
- The principles of active learning can also be seen as creative, thereby providing teachers with an opportunity to model creativity to learners and to emphasise the importance of creativity in learning.

Further reading

Beghetto, R.A. and Kaufman, J.C. (2014) 'Classroom contexts for creativity', *High Ability Studies*, 25 (1): 53–69.
You can read this if you are interested in exploring more ways of embedding creativity in your classroom.

Swiderski, S.M. (2011) 'Transforming principles into practice: Using cognitive active learning strategies in the high school classroom', *The Clearing House: A Journal of Educational Strategies, Issues and Ideas*, 84 (6): 239–43.
This is useful for a more detailed exploration of cognitive active learning.

Bibliography

Beghetto, R.A. and Kaufman, J.C. (2014) 'Classroom contexts for creativity', *High Ability Studies*, 25 (1): 53–69.

Braund, M. (2015) 'Drama and learning science: An empty space?', *British Educational Research Journal*, 41 (1): 102–21.

Bruner, J. (1962) 'The conditions of creativity', in H. Gruber, G. Terrell, and M. Wertheimer, (eds), *Contemporary Approaches to Creative Thinking*. New York: Atherton.

Cropley, A. and Urban, K. (2000) 'Programs and strategies for nurturing creativity', in K.A. Heller, F.J. Monks, R.J. Sternberg and R. Subotnik (eds), *The International Handbook of Giftedness and Talent* (online). Oxford: Elsevier. (accessed 30 December 2017).

Csikszentmihalyi, M. and Wolfe, R. (2000) 'New conceptions and research approaches to creativity: Implications of a systems perspective for creativity in education', in K.A. Heller, F.J. Monks, R.J. Sternberg and R. Subotnik (eds), *The International Handbook of Giftedness and Talent*. Oxford: Elsevier.

Flowerday, T. and Shell, D.F. (2015) 'Disentangling the effects of interest and choice on learning, engagement, and attitude', *Learning and Individual Differences*, 40 (5): 134–40.

González-Cutre, D., Sicilia, Á., Sierra, A., Ferriz, R. and Hagger, M. (2016) 'Understanding the need for novelty from the perspective of self-determination theory', *Personality and Individual Differences*, 102: 159–69.

Harackiewicz, J.M. et al. (2008) 'The role of achievement goals in the development of interest: Reciprocal relations between achievement goals, interest and performance', *Journal of Educational Psychology*, 100 (1): 105–22.

Heathcote, D. and Herbert, P. (1985) 'A drama of learning: Mantle of the expert', *Theory Into Practice*, 24 (3): 173–80.

Johnson, E.C., Liu, K. and Goble, K. (2015) 'Mantle of the Expert: Integrating dramatic inquiry and visual arts in social studies', *Social Studies*, 106 (5): 204–8.

Kaufman, J.C. and Beghetto, R.A (2009) 'Beyond big and little: The Four C model of creativity', *Review of General Psychology*, 13 (1): 1–12.

Lauber, L. (2007) 'Role play: Principles to increase effectiveness', in M.L. Silberman (ed.), *The Handbook of Experiential Learning*. San Franciso, CA: Pfeiffer.

Lipstein, R. and Renninger, K.A. (2007) 'Putting things into words: 12–15-year-old students' interest for writing', in P. Boscolo and S. Hidi (eds), *Motivation and Writing: Research and School Practice*. New York: Kluwer Academic/Plenum Press.

Markey, A. and Loewenstein, G. (2014) 'Curiosity', in R. Pekrun and L. Linnenbrink-Garcia (eds.) *International Handbook of Emotions in Education*. Routledge: New York.

McQueen, H. (2014) *Roles, Rights, and Responsibilities in UK Education*. New York: Palgrave Macmillan.

Nebel, S., Schneider, S. and Rey, G.D. (2016) 'Mining learning and crafting scientific experiments: A literature review on the use of Minecraft in education and research', *Educational Technology & Society*, 19 (2): 355–66.

Nolen, S.B. (2007) 'The role of literature communities in the development of children's interest in writing', in S. Hidi and P. Boscolo (eds), *Writing and Motivation*. Oxford: Elsevier.

Ødegaard, M. (2003) 'Dramatic science: A critical review of drama in science education', *Studies in Science Education*, 39 (1): 75–101.

Quinn, C. (2007) 'Computer-based simulations: Principles of engagement', in M.L. Silberman (ed.), *The Handbook of Experiential Learning*. San Francisco, CA: Pfeiffer.

Renniger, K.A. and Hidi, S. (2016) *The Power of Interest for Motivation and Engagement*. Abingdon: Routledge.

Rotgans, J.I. and Schmidt, H.G. (2014) 'Situational interest and learning: Thirst for knowledge' in *Learning and Instruction*, 32: 37–50.

Ryan and Deci (2000) 'Self-determination theory and the facilitation of intrinsic motivation, social development, and well-being', *American Psychologist*, 55 (1): 68–78.

Ryan, R.M. and Deci, E.L. (2006) 'Self-regulation and the problem of human autonomy: Does psychology need choice, self-determination, and will?' *Journal of Personality*, 74 (6): 1557–86.

Swiderski, S.M. (2011) 'Transforming principles into practice: Using cognitive active learning strategies in the high school classroom', *The Clearing House: A Journal of Educational Strategies, Issues and Ideas*, 84 (6): 239–43.

Thomas, T.G. (2009) 'Active learning', E.F. Provenzo and A.B. Provenzo (eds), *Encyclopedia of the Social and Cultural Foundations of Education*. Thousand Oaks, CA: Sage.

Zusak, M. (2005) *The Book Thief*. New York: Alfred A. Knopf.

10

EMPOWERING LEARNERS

Chapter guide

In this chapter, you will learn about:

- Definitions of empowerment

- How to improve and maintain learning through pedagogies of empowerment

- How to share responsibility and accountability between teachers and pupils

- Lifelong learning: Building learning for life in pupils

- Empowering school structures: Including pupils and teachers in school decision-making

As we approach the end of this book, we turn our attention to a complex and often slippery concept: 'empowerment'. Whereas for some, empowerment is merely another, perhaps generalised, term for motivation (Frymier et al., 1996), for others, empowerment represents a whole range of motivational processes that facilitate initial engagement with a task, continued motivation towards it, and finally, positive feelings associated with the task and the motivational process itself (Conger and Kanungo, 1988).

In Chapter 7, we explored how some of the theories of motivation outlined in Chapter 3 can be applied to classroom practice in order to move pupils towards intrinsic motivational behaviours. In this chapter, we will begin by exploring some of the definitions of empowerment, drawing a distinction between motivation and empowerment. Next, we will introduce some practical strategies that can be used to empower learners both within the classroom and in the wider school context. Finally, we will consider the potential of these pedagogies of empowerment to help build a transformative education system that sees high-quality education and high levels of well-being as inextricably linked.

How does empowerment fit in with motivation?

Ryan and Deci's (2000) self-determination continuum maps different types of motivation and accompanying regulatory styles, moving from a state of amotivation, through extrinsic motivation, to intrinsic motivation. Although Ryan and Deci are clear that the continuum is not developmental (people don't move from one regulatory stage to the next in tidy, sequential jumps), it is still useful to explore how the different regulatory styles within the continuum can be evidenced within the classroom in order to make these visible within our educational experiences (Table 10.1).

Table 10.1 Continuum of motivation, adapted from Ryan and Deci (2000)

Type of motivation (locus of causality)	Regulatory style	What does this look like in the classroom?
Amotivation (impersonal)	Non-regulation	A learner sees themselves as lacking competence, value and control within their learning, and therefore has no motivation whatsoever
Extrinsic motivation (external)	External regulation	A learner follows explicit rules within the classroom in a bid to comply and receive external rewards or avoid external punishments
Extrinsic motivation (somewhat external)	Introjected regulation	A learner uses self-control in order to follow rules, based on a partial acceptance of the external regulation. This type of motivation is associated with internal rewards such as feelings of pride and internal punishments such as feelings of guilt
Extrinsic motivation (somewhat internal)	Identified regulation	A learner values the goals or regulations put in place by the teacher and sees it as important to follow these
Extrinsic motivation (internal)	Integrated regulation	A learner completely embraces the identified regulations associated with the previous type of motivation as part of the 'self', and therefore follows these willingly and with whole-hearted commitment. This type of motivation differs from the next type, intrinsic motivation, in that the learner is still focusing on attaining particular external outcomes instead of being motivated intrinsically

Type of motivation (locus of causality)	Regulatory style	What does this look like in the classroom?
Intrinsic motivation (internal)	Intrinsic regulation	A learner self-directs their learning, motivated by inherent interest and enjoyment

Whilst we have explored some of Ryan and Deci's extrinsic motivation types earlier in this book (Chapter 3), it is important to take stock here of the differences between the most autonomous motivation type in the extrinsic motivation category (integrated regulation) and intrinsic motivation itself. Ryan and Deci highlight that many of the manifestations of these two types of motivation can be very similar, making it difficult to establish whether a learner is internally extrinsically motivated or intrinsically motivated. The crucial difference is that the former is underpinned by identification with the aspects of the regulatory system in place and a wholehearted acceptance of its rationale and requirements that then results in a complete commitment to upholding these. Crucially, this type of motivation requires an underlying regulatory system to which the learner has been exposed, as well as the exposition of its requirements and the reasons behind these, so that the learner can fully identify with this pre-existing system.

In contrast, intrinsic motivation is internally regulated and self-motivated, inspired by a love of learning. Due to the focus here on learning for its own sake, rather than for any external reward, intrinsic motivation is sometimes also described as emotional engagement with a particular task or academic interest. Ryan and Deci (2000) see intrinsic motivation as a key aspect of psychological well-being, and theorists have seen intrinsic motivation as having a positive relationship with a variety of aspects of academic success (Froiland and Worrell, 2016).

If intrinsic motivation is an admirable goal for any learner, and is seen as likely to support their academic achievements and psychological well-being, then why is empowerment important? Surely, if a learner can reach a state of intrinsic motivation, then they are a happy, successful human beings and our work as educators is done? Perhaps. But perhaps not. Whereas intrinsic motivation is rooted in self-determination and enjoyment of the learning process, empowerment focuses on enabling learners to act within their environment.

Empowerment, then, could perhaps be seen as the next level of Ryan and Deci's (2000) continuum, where a learner takes control of their own learning and becomes the master of their own education. Whereas intrinsic motivation is associated with self-direction, the actions associated with empowerment are stronger than this and link to concepts such as power and authority.

What is empowerment?

We have begun by situating empowerment within self-determination theory and considering how this links to Ryan and Deci's (2000) motivation
continuum so that we can start to see empowerment as a step beyond
intrinsic motivation. We now turn to some precise definitions of empowerment so that we can begin to deepen our understanding of its nature and
harness aspects of empowerment within our classrooms and schools.

Management theorists Conger and Kanungo see the importance of perceived personal competency as opposed to achieved performance outcomes
in their definition of empowerment:

> Empowering means enabling and it implies raising subordinates'
> convictions in their own effectiveness (successfully executing desired
> behaviour) rather than raising subordinates' hopes for favourable
> performance outcomes. (1988: 476)

Although the use of the term 'subordinates' is somewhat uncomfortable
in the twenty-first century, Conger and Kanungo's (1988) definition demonstrates that empowerment is not the same as simply fulfilling goals for the
sake of achieving extrinsic rewards, but that it is rooted in the individual's
perceived efficacy and therefore is grounded in the three conditions of self-
determination theory: personal growth, autonomy and interconnectedness.

Thomas and Velthouse (1990) sought to build on Conger and Kanungo's
(1988) definition of empowerment by conflating the concept with intrinsic
task motivation. Sounds familiar. Thomas and Velthouse summarise some
of the different ways in which empowerment can be perceived here:

> To empower means to give power to. Power, however, has several
> meanings. In a legal sense, power means authority, so that empower-
> ment can mean authorization. Power also may be used to describe
> capacity, as in the self-efficacy definition of Conger and Kanungo.
> However, power also means energy. Thus, to empower also can mean
> to energise. (1990: 667)

Here, Thomas and Velthouse see the energy associated with the word
'power' as reflecting a new management style that embraces intrinsic task
motivation as a way of maximising worker productivity and a key aspect of
a successful, empowering management style. Whilst Thomas and Velthouse's
thoughtful development of a model of empowerment is useful from a managerial perspective, the tendency to focus on 'empowering workers with
respect to a given task' (ibid.: 679) does not harmonise with our view of
empowerment for learners as a more transformative, holistic process.

Instead, the focus on the completion of a particular task arguably fits with definitions of certain types of motivation more convincingly than with definitions of empowerment. We can tell a student that we want to empower them to read a book, but is the use of 'empower' here truly accurate? We might want to encourage them to read a book, or motivate them to read a book. If we argue that by gently coercing them to pick up a text and scan through it is empowering just because we have used the verb 'empower', then we are dismissing the true potential of empowerment in education by misinterpreting its meaning, scope and potential impact.

Perhaps more usefully, Zimmerman (1995) defines 'psychological empowerment' as the process of gaining mastery over issues of concern, drawing an important distinction between empowering processes and empowered outcomes. Empowering processes are the experiences in which:

> individuals learn to see a closer correspondence between their goals and a sense of how to achieve them, gain greater access to and control over resources, and where people, organizations, and communities gain mastery over their lives. (Ibid.: 583)

In contrast, Zimmerman explains that empowered outcomes are the indicators of empowerment that can be measured, which are organised into three categories:

- The intrapersonal component of psychological empowerment involves the ways that individuals think about themselves, for example their perceived ability level in the face of a particular task or their sense of self-efficacy.
- The interactional component refers to the way that an individual understands their community or sociopolitical context, and how they subsequently use decision-making skills in order to mediate between their own intrapersonal beliefs and the wider contexts in which they exist.
- The behavioural component refers to the actions that an individual takes in order to exert control within their contexts. (1995: 588)

Zimmerman (1995) highlights that the interactions between different factors within each category are highly complex and difficult to capture. However, we can use Zimmerman's framework as a starting point for considering empowerment within a school context (Figure 10.1).

Having theorised key aspects of psychological empowerment, Zimmerman has also collaboratively devised a youth education programme that focuses on empowering young people (Franzen et al., 2009; Zimmerman et al., 2017). Although this makes use of extracurricular learning opportunities

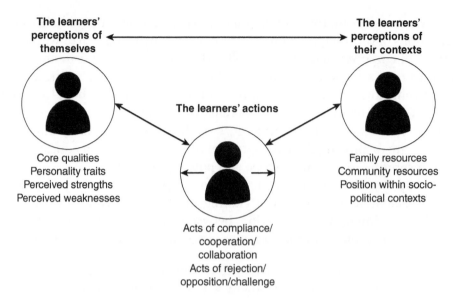

Figure 10.1   Diagram based on Zimmerman (1995)

rather than formal schooling, Zimmerman et al. outline how the Youth Empowerment Solutions (YES) programme 'is responsive to local culture, creates opportunities for intergenerational collaboration, and prepares youth to plan and implement community change that they would like to see' (2017: 2). The positioning of the young participants is crucial here, in that they are actively engaging with their community rather than simply being informed about the issues it faces. In devising the programme with an active learning approach, Zimmerman et al. (2011) found that learners preferred active pedagogies as these enabled them to exert more control over the classroom environment, echoing the spirit of the empowerment programme itself.

Zimmerman et al. provide further explanation of some of the features of empowerment in an educational setting:

> Empowering processes are ones in which opportunities to increase capabilities and confidence, learn and practice skills, exert control, and influence decisions are fundamental . . . A process is empowering if it helps youth develop the cognitive and behavioral skills necessary to critically understand their social environments and become independent problem solvers and decision makers. (ibid.: 426)

This raises a crucial point as we deepen our understanding of empowerment: empowerment is not about surrendering all adult authority and promoting child-led anarchy, but in fact is about guiding our learners through different processes in order for them to become fully and meaningfully empowered within different contexts. As part of these processes, learners will require greater autonomy in order to be able to meaningfully exercise their own agency and interact with their environments through their own actions, but this is not the first step in creating an empowering education system.

MEANINGFUL GOALS

A key aspect of Zimmerman's concept of psychological empowerment is that individuals need to experience empowering processes that enable them to work towards achieving their goals and develop their access to and mastery of resources. It is useful to consider how far learners are already able to do this within our current educational settings:

- Consider what 'goal-setting' means in your school. Do learners set meaningful goals based on their own life ambitions and aspirations? How far does 'goal-setting' focus on performance outcomes like achieving a particular grade in a test?
- Consider the resources that learners have access to in your school. This does not just refer to those created by the teacher or teaching assistant, but more broadly relates to all the possible tools that a learner could utilise. The expertise of another adult or the consultation of a reference book could be examples. Are learners given the opportunity to identify, select and evaluate the resources on offer? Are they eventually guided through this process over time? Are they given the opportunity to do so independently?
- How could you build the following elements of psychological empowerment into your classroom?

Intrapersonal understanding of the self

- Meaningful goal-setting
- Opportunities to explore personal identity

Interpersonal understanding of wider contexts

- Identification, application and evaluation of social resources (e.g., giving learners the opportunity to use their skills effectively and to guide others in this process)
- Identification, application and evaluation of other resources (e.g., particular tools that can support learning)

(Continued)

(Continued)

- Opportunities to explore different contexts and the opportunities that these afford the learner (e.g., their family environment, their friendship network, their school community)

Understanding of personal behaviour and consequences

- Opportunities to choose specific actions that are not always directed by an adult
- Opportunities to reflect on the consequences of actions (this often characterises an approach to negative behaviours in school, but why should such reflection always be negative?)
- Planning how to achieve small-scale, meaningful learning goals
- Implementing planned actions and reflecting on their success or failure
- Evaluating the appropriateness or effectiveness of actions in a learning context

CASE STUDY

In a primary school in the East Midlands, learners in Year 3 are introduced to a variety of mathematical tools (numicon, cubes, bead strings, etc.) over the course of the year, with explicit instruction on how to use these in order to support their understanding. By the end of the autumn term, the learners are encouraged to self-select from the available resources based on personal preference and appropriateness, which gives them the opportunity to choose resources on a 'trial-and-error' basis and, in turn, develop their ability to make informed, purposeful decisions.

Whilst this could be seen as a relatively minor aspect of the school experience, the learners are actually being taught some of the skills necessary to achieve psychological empowerment through the focus on selection, application and evaluation of resources. Alongside this, the learners also develop a deeper understanding of what is actually required of them within the context of each particular mathematical concept. This arguably represents increasing understanding of their interpersonal context as a learner within a formal school setting, as they are given the opportunity to engage more deeply with mathematics and what is required of them in the mathematics classroom by independently analysing particular problems and then independently strategising how best to solve them.

Embedded into the wider school curriculum and culture, a greater emphasis on opportunities for developing learning as an empowering process could result in increased feelings of empowerment for young people in schools.

Moving towards an empowering school

Kirk et al. (2016) build on Zimmerman's definition of empowerment specifically within a school setting:

> In schools, this process [of empowerment] occurs as disempowered students gain the power needed to meet their individual needs (e.g., learning, social relationships, diploma) and work with others (e.g., students, teachers, administrators) to achieve collective goals. (Ibid.: 589)

Kirt et al. continue to outline a number of key aspects of an empowering school setting, including:

- Shared power and decision-making
- Positive sense of community
- Quality activities
- Mutual goals
- Equitable teacher–student roles
- Positive student–teacher relationships. (2016: 590)

A collective ethos of mutual respect and equity clearly underpins this approach to empowering learners. As such, it is important to turn our attention to the relationships between teachers and students and how these can best be used to empower learners.

Empowerment and the teacher–student relationship

We have already discussed some aspects of the teacher–student relationship in terms of behaviour for learning in Chapter 4. We will now use Engeström's (2001) basic activity model from cultural-historical activity theory to explore the interaction between teachers and students in the classroom (Figure 10.2).

If we see the basic activity model (or triangle) on the left as representing the learner and the model (or triangle) on the right as representing the teacher, then we can begin to analyse some of the key aspects of their classroom activity.

Turning our attention to the learner (or subject) first, we can see that the lines in the diagram represent the interactions between a number of different aspects of the individual's experience and social context. 'Mediating artifacts' refer to the tools available to the subject in striving to achieve their

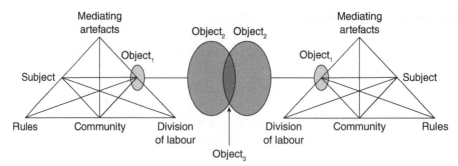

Figure 10.2 Engeström's activity model (2001) reprinted by permission of the publisher, Taylor & Francis Ltd, http://www.tandfonline.com

goal or Object 1. 'Rules' refer to the sociocultural norms dictating their behaviour, in this case the rules explicitly and implicitly enforced for learners within the classroom. 'Community' refers to the learner's classmates, for example their possible friendship groups within the class, their role within the teacher–student community or their membership of the wider school community. Finally, 'division of labour' refers to 'who does what' within this context, for instance the learner will probably be responsible for completing classwork set by the teacher, etc.

If we now move to the teacher as subject, the mediating artifacts might refer to their prior knowledge of a particular concept that they wish to teach, their ability to research this topic in more detail and their understanding of pedagogical approaches. The rules by which the teacher is governed are legal, but there are also likely to be rules that are set by the school in which the teacher works. Like the learner, the teacher also exists within the teacher–student community, as well as within a wider community of teachers within the school and an even wider professional community of teachers, perhaps subscribing to a particular ideological perspective on education. The teacher could also perhaps be a member of the same geographical community as the learner if they live in the same area. Finally, the teacher's role in the division of labour may focus on their providing information, explaining a particular task and then checking the learner's understanding of that task in some way.

The object in the model refers to the goal of the activity being represented, which can be transformed into an outcome. The transition from Object 1 to Object 2 reflects the move towards a collectively understood goal rooted in the interaction between the two individuals. This may then be followed by the collective negotiation of Object 3, a potentially shared, mutually constructed goal. In this way, the goal of the activity can shift quickly and is not static. There are some interesting implications of this model for education, with Song and Kim (2016) exploring teacher motivation and Gade (2015) exploring teacher–researcher collaboration. For us, the model can be useful to illuminate some interesting activity interactions between teachers and students that can then be linked to empowerment.

The shifting nature of the objects involved in Engeström's model highlights the potentially shifting nature of the teacher's and student's goals within any given activity. For instance, a student's object may be to please their teacher in order to develop a positive working relationship with them. In doing so, the student may also seek to complete their classwork to the best of their ability as they perceive this as a 'tool' through which they can gain the positive regard of their teacher. This largely unseen, interpersonal goal of teacher–student interactions could tentatively be proposed as a partial explanation for findings such as those from Hallinan that 'teachers who support their students by caring about them and by respecting and praising them satisfy students' needs and, in so doing, increase students' attachment to school' (2008: 282). If some learners exhibit positive behaviours due to their desire to establish and maintain a positive relationship with their teacher rather than solely aiming to comply with school rules or to achieve academically, then arguably, their cooperation is rooted in a positive environment of mutual respect and positive regard.

There are also some important implications here for empowerment. By its nature, empowerment in education may require increased independence for learners in order for them to truly develop mastery over their lives. If we consider how this model would look if the object of the learner was to achieve psychological empowerment and the object of the teacher was to empower the learner, then there may be initial conflicts between these goals and other aspects of the model, such as the rules, community and division of labour. Even though the teacher and student have a shared goal, the social, cultural and historical contexts in which they are situated may not facilitate the fulfilment of this.

For instance, a teacher may want to encourage independence for a group of older students by removing a series of school-determined deadlines for the completion of individual homework tasks. The teacher may want the students to learn to manage their own time outside of the classroom (aiding their understanding of how to utilise a key learning resource) and therefore sets a minimum number of tasks that should be completed within the timeframe but does not dictate when each individual task should be completed. The teacher may come into contact with a variety of obstacles within our activity model. First, the learners may perceive the teacher as reneging on some of their responsibilities as part of the division of labour, with them perhaps usually being associated with helping learners to organise themselves. Similarly, the relevant communities in which the teacher exists may take a dim view of their decision, perhaps based on prior experience or cultural norms. Perhaps most significantly, the teacher may not be allowed to take this action due to the rules in place within their school. In this way, the model can help us to identify potential obstacles to empowerment that would otherwise have been less visible.

According to Engeström, these types of contradictions can build up over time within an activity system:

> When an activity system adopts a new element from the outside (for example, a new technology or a new object), it often leads to an aggravated secondary contradiction where some old element (for example, the rules or the division of labor) collides with the new one. (2001: 137)

Crucially, these contradictions (and the conflicts that they can cause) can lead to transformation of the activity model itself. In this way, the tensions within the activity model can build up and cause individuals to question aspects of their social world, enacting a process of change which arguably could lead to their own empowerment.

Authority and empowerment

The difficulties that teachers may face in adopting pedagogies of empowerment highlight one of the key concerns about proposing empowerment as a goal of our education system. In empowering learners, teachers (and their managers or leaders) may be concerned about the increasing agency of young people and what they may see as the decreasing authority of adults within the school context.

Many teachers and schools are concerned about the behaviour of young people and rightly strive to maintain safe, supportive environments (see Chapter 4). For many, the teacher's authority is a key factor in reducing the risk of danger and disruption. As such, it is worth briefly turning our attention to perspectives on authority in education in order to address these concerns. Bingham (2008) proposes that authority is a relational rather than fixed phenomenon, and that it is dialogic (many-voiced) rather than monologic (one-voiced). Turning his back on Kant's conception of authority as something to be submitted to or asserted over others, Bingham argues that 'authority relations can lead to domination and submission, or they can lead to reciprocity and agency' (ibid.: 15).

Bingham engages with traditional perspectives of authority in education and explains how many traditionalists see authority as an essential possession of the teacher, afforded by their position within the school organisation and their learnedness. He contrasts this with a progressive rejection of authority that is rooted in a belief that authority and social justice are incompatible. Bingham also explains the perspective of critical-ists who see teacher authority as a means to an end if this enables learning to take place and therefore produces social justice. He criticises the per-spectives of all three as they see authority as a substance that is bestowed on those in positions of power rather than an aspect of relation. Bingham's viewpoint stands up to examples from the classroom. It would be difficult to argue that all teachers have natural authority when they are directly challenged by negative behaviours from students; for instance, the teacher who desperately tells a student to stop dancing on the table and kicking his or her classmates is arguably lacking authority at that moment in time. How can this authority have been lost when most perspectives see author-ity as a fixed substance that is possessed by some and not others? Bingham's view of authority as relational provides a convincing explanation for such instances.

If we draw on Bingham's view that authority is not a fixed substance pos-sessed by teachers in the first place, then we see that the argument that teachers may lose authority by empowering learners is a misconception. Authority is not something to be fought over in the classroom. Bingham elaborates on this:

> There must be an oscillation, on the part of the teacher, between being in control and letting loose. And there must also be such an oscillation on the side of the student too. For recognition [of the student as a subject with agency] to count, the student must know that the teacher is predictable enough not be threatening. Yet, the teacher must seem autonomous enough not to *have to* grant recognition. Recognition counts for the one recognized only when there is the option, on the part of the one recognizing, of not recognizing. (2008: 143)

Bingham draws on a range of psychoanalytical perspectives in order to illustrate this conception of authority, highlighting the complexity of ana-lysing the relationships between teachers and students. In arguing that relational authority is circuitous, Bingham's oscillation between control and letting loose would be visible within different classroom-based versions of Engeström's activity model. This loosening of authority can, in fact, be seen in the example we explored previously, relating to the teacher changing the way that homework is handed in so as to promote increasing autonomy in their learners, with the learners having to adjust to this recognition of themselves as subjects with agency rather than objects to be controlled by the teacher. Crucially, the teacher has decided to give their learners greater autonomy over an aspect of the curriculum that can be affected by issues such as lack of completion, plagiarism and varying levels of effort from different learners. As Warton argues, 'literature on the link between homework and the attainment of these [lifelong learning] skills is particularly sparse' (2001: 158). The teacher has made a conscious decision to give students greater autonomy over an area of their education over which they already have a greater degree of control than others, although their decision to exercise this control (for instance, by completing or not completing their homework) is usually followed by an extrinsic reward or sanction. The risk here then is arguably low stakes, in that the teacher risks non-completion whenever they set a homework task and can therefore afford to experiment with a different approach to homework, which focuses on giving the learners the opportunity to act independently and subsequently to face the consequences of those actions.

CASE STUDY

We have already referred to a secondary school teacher experimenting with homework in this chapter, but will now give further detail about this practical example.

A secondary school English teacher wanted to help learners in Year 12 to develop their time-management skills and to exercise autonomy in completing homework. The teacher devised a 'takeaway homework' menu (these types of resources are common across schools and many educators take responsibility for inventing or popularising these, including Ross Morrison McGill, 2013) that featured a range of optional, open-ended tasks. The teacher specified that the learners should complete at least three of the tasks by the end of that half-term. Tasks ranged from creating a board game that would help a learner to understand key aspects of William Shakespeare's *Othello*, Thomas Hardy's *Tess of the d'Urbervilles* (1892 [1891]) or Arthur Miller's *Death of a Salesman* (1996 [1949]), to scripting and producing a podcast for revision of one or more of these three texts. A crucial aspect of the teacher's strategy, however, was that the completion of the homework would coincide with a 'takeaway homework party' in which learners would exhibit their completed homework and reflect on how it had helped their progress.

The homework produced by the learners was of an incredible standard. A group of learners collaborated in order to script, film and edit a reality TV-style documentary about *Tess of the d'Urbervilles*, interviewing key characters in a local woodland that doubled as 'The Chase' in Hardy's Wessex. Another student produced a Monopoly-style board game that rated various settings in the novel by their tragic intensity in order to assign them monetary value, and featured 'Cards of Misfortune' rather than 'Chance' cards. One student (who rarely completed homework tasks and struggled to manage time effectively) choreographed and performed a dance inspired by the novel, with various movements representing key recurring motifs such as birds. There were still learners who had left their tasks until the last minute and crammed their efforts into a few hours the night before, but greeted with the creativity and pride of their classmates during the homework party, they self-censured, and the levels of commitment and effort of all the students increased over the course of the year as the strategy was embedded.

Empowerment and social justice

Engeström's activity model and our discussion of its potential to capture change-making processes in education provides a tantalising glimpse into one possible version of the future of education. If teachers and learners aim for empowerment, address the subsequent tensions within the activity model and enact collective change, then education could rapidly evolve in ways that we may not even be able to fully conceive at this stage.

It is crucial then to consider the impact that a transformative, empowering model of education could have on a key concern within contemporary education: social inequality. There are many groups of learners who can be seen as underachieving within education systems across the world, from Aboriginal students in Canada (Levin, 2009) to white, working-class learners in the UK (Demie and Lewis, 2011). Arguably, if the aim of education for students and teachers shifts to focus on empowerment rather than academic success for extrinsic reward, then the activity model will adapt to any structural tensions that this creates. The use of the activity model also necessitates a focus on the wider social and cultural contexts of the individual student, rather than tying their achievement solely to their intrapersonal qualities. Goodman and Burton highlight how the government focuses on performance outcomes and data 'serves to exacerbate the cycle of poor performance, weak self-esteem and low teacher expectations which, along with structural mechanisms such as setting make it increasingly difficult for pupils to improve' (2012: 511). By embracing the goal of empowerment, identifying structural tensions through the activity model and allowing teachers and students the autonomy to adapt accordingly rather than constraining them to previous rules, divisions of labour and even communities, our educational systems could evolve beyond the structural mechanisms that result in attainment gaps between disadvantaged and advantaged learners.

If we, as teachers, can relieve or even just ignore at least some of our fears of change, then we could be part of something truly momentous: a transformative education system.

Chapter summary

There are many definitions of 'empowerment'. We see it as a step beyond intrinsic motivation, where the empowered learner begins to interact with their environment in order to achieve their goals. This builds on Zimmerman's (1995) definition of psychological empowerment:

- Kirk et al. argue that the following are key aspects of an empowering school setting:
  o Shared power and decision-making
  o Positive sense of community
  o Quality activities
  o Mutual goals
  o Equitable student–teacher roles
  o Positive student–teacher relationships. (2016: 590)
- Engeström's activity model can help us to explore how the process of empowering learners can look in practice and some of the obstacles that may be faced. The activity model features the following concepts:
  o The subject – or person involved in the activity
  o Mediating artifacts – or the tools available to the subject in striving to achieve their goal or object
  o The object – or goal of the activity
  o Rules – or the sociocultural norms implicitly or explicitly governing behaviour
  o Community – or the people involved in the activity
  o Division of labour – or 'who does what' within the activity. (2001: 135)
- Some teachers may fear that in empowering their learners, they inadvertently compromise their own authority as classroom teachers. We draw on Bingham's view that authority is relational (2008) rather than something inherent within the role of the teacher and lacking within the role of the student. In this way, the increased agency of the learner should not be perceived as a threat to the authority of the teacher.
- An education system focused on empowerment could have transformative potential, in that it embraces change rather than reinforcing society's pre-existing structural inequalities within a school context. This could afford significant benefits to learners, who are arguably disadvantaged within the education system currently.

Further reading

Goodman, R. and Burton, D. (2012) 'What is the nature of the achievement gap, why does it persist and are government goals sufficient to create social justice in the education system?', *Education 3-13*, 40 (5): 500–14.
For a more detailed exploration of some of the challenges facing disadvantaged pupils, read this.

Lee, A.N. and Nie, Y. (2017) 'Teachers' perceptions of school leaders' empowering behaviours and psychological empowerment: Evidence from a Singapore sample', *Educational Management Administration & Leadership*, 45 (2): 260–83.
If you are interested in the empowerment of teachers as well as learners then you may want to read this article.

Bibliography

Bingham, C. (2008) *Authority is Relational: Rethinking Educational Empowerment*. Albany, NY: State University of New York Press.

Conger, J.A. and Kanungo, R.N. (1988) 'The empowerment process: Integrating theory and practice', *Academy of Management Review*, 13 (3): 471–82.

Demie, F. and Lewis, K. (2011) 'White working-class achievement: An ethnographic study of barriers to learning in schools', *Educational Studies*, 37 (3): 245–64.

Engeström, Y. (2001) 'Expansive learning at work: Toward an activity theoretical reconceptualization', *Journal of Education and Work*, 14 (1): 133–56.

Franzen, S. , Morrel-Samuels, S., Reischl, T.M. and Zimmerman, M.A. (2009) 'Using process evaluation to strengthen intergenerational partnerships in the Youth Empowerment Solutions program', *Journal of Prevention & Intervention in the Community*, 37 (4): 289–301.

Froiland, J.M. and Worrell, F.C. (2016) 'Intrinsic motivation, learning goals, engagement, and achievement in a diverse high school', *Psychology in the Schools*, 13 (3): 471–82.

Frymier, A.B., Shulman, G. and Houser, M. (1996) 'The development of a learner empowerment measure', *Communication Education*, 45 (3): 181–99.

Gade, S. (2015) 'Unpacking teacher–researcher collaboration with three theoretical frameworks: A case of expansive learning activity?', *Cultural Studies of Science Education*, 10 (3): 603–19.

Goodman, R. and Burton, D. (2012) 'What is the nature of the achievement gap, why does it persist and are government goals sufficient to create social justice in the education system?', *Education 3-13*, 40 (5): 500–14.

Hallinan, M.T. (2008) 'Teacher influences on students' attachment to school', *Sociology of Education*, 81 (3): 271–83.

Hardy, T. (1892 [1891]) *Tess of the d'Urbervilles*. Boston, MA: James R. Osgood, McIlvaine & Co.

Kirk, C.M. et al. (2016) 'The power of student empowerment: Measuring classroom predictors and individual indicators', *Journal of Educational Research*, 109 (6): 589–95.

Lee, A.N. and Nie, Y. (2017) 'Teachers' perceptions of school leaders' empowering behaviours and psychological empowerment: Evidence from a Singapore sample', *Educational Management Administration & Leadership*, 45 (2): 260–83.

Levin, B. (2009) 'Aboriginal education still needs work', *Phi Delta Kappan*, 90 (9): 689–90.

Miller, A. (1996 [1949]) *Death of a Salesman*. Harmondsworth: Penguin Books.

Morrison McGill, R. (2013) *100 Ideas for Secondary Teachers: Outstanding Lessons*. London: Bloomsbury.

Ryan, R.M. and Deci, E.L. (2000) 'Self-determination theory and the facilitation of intrinsic motivation, social development, and well-being', *American Psychologist*, 55 (1): 68–78.

Song, B. and Kim, T.-Y. (2016) 'Teacher (de)motivation from an activity theory perspective: Cases of two experienced EFL teachers in South Korea', *System*, 57: 134–45.

Thomas, K.W. and Velthouse, B.A. (1990) 'Cognitive elements of empowerment: An "interpretive" model of intrinsic task motivation', *Academy of Management Review*, 15 (4): 666–81.

Warton, P.M. (2001) 'The forgotten voices in homework: Views of students', *Educational Psychologist*, 36 (3): 155–65.

Zimmerman, M.A. (1995) 'Psychological empowerment: Issues and illustrations', *American Journal of Community Psychology*, 23 (5): 581–99.

Zimmerman, M.A. et al. (2011) 'Youth Empowerment Solutions for Peaceful Communities: Combining theory and practice in a community-level violence prevention curriculum', *Health Promotion Practice*, 12 (3): 425–39.

Zimmerman, M.A. et al. (2017) 'Youth Empowerment Solutions: Evaluation of an after-school program to engage middle school students in community change', *Health Education and Behavior*, 45 (4): 1–12.

11

THE FUTURE

What do we stand for in education?

Our values as early career teachers: Staying the distance

We place values and humanity at the centre of our approach to education – both for the teachers and their pupils. High standards of learning should be expected of all learners. High values must be enshrined in a good education. This is equally important for early career teachers. By high values, we mean:

Integrity: Educationally sound processes and outcomes that are built on morally and professionally defensible foundations.

Agency: Ownership and control of the learning process by both pupils and teachers, which ensures that learners are able to take responsibility and develop independence in their learning.

Validity: Educationally justifiable approaches to teaching and learning that are located in a broad evidence base.

Mutuality: Educationally shared experiences, aims and outcomes that recognise the relationship between learning and teaching outcomes for both pupils and the professional development and growth of teachers.

Equity: High-quality learning that is valued as a right for both pupils and teachers. In fact, pupils have a right to be educated by appropriately qualified, trained and continually growing professionals.

Whilst we do not always agree with all the details of Rogers (1963b), his ideas do have some resonance. Rogers (ibid.) sees learning as an active, constructive experience, linked to the self-concepts of those involved. He views anything that challenges the self-concept of the learning as being detrimental to their education (Rogers, 1963a). We do believe that 'challenge' is vitally important for both teachers and pupils. Whilst we have placed great emphasis on the role of self-regulation and self-direction in the education of teachers and pupils, we believe that the teacher is critical in developing learning in the classroom. Whilst the teacher can function as 'facilitator' in a lesson, their role is more significant. Teachers do make a difference in what children learn, how they learn and how motivated they feel in a lesson (Schunk et al., 2012). But we cannot take teachers for granted. Teachers are human beings and have doubts and questions about their performance and role in school much like learners do (Rogers, 1963a). Zee and Koomen (2016) explain that teacher self-efficacy, pupil outcomes and the well-being of both are connected. Csikszentmihalyi's (1990) concept of 'flow' can be applied to teacher learning just as it can be applied to that of children. For teachers to experience flow in the classroom, it is quite likely that the learners will be just as involved in the activities as are the teachers. In fact, we could argue that 'flow' in the classroom is as much about the timeless experience of engagement in learning as it is about the fluid nature of learning and control over learning by the pupil and the teacher. A high-quality classroom experience is empowering for both pupils and teachers. 'Flow' therefore is not only a psychological concept, but it also has political undertones in terms of the distribution of power and control in the learning process. Agency or the degree of control over the learning process is an important psychological as well as political reality. We argue that both pupils and their teachers must demonstrate 'agentive' learning in the classroom and in their development as a teacher. If 'agency' is the capacity to act in the learning process, then it is important that both pupils and teachers are provided with the freedom to act, that there is an expectation of active learning and that learners should take responsibility for exercising 'agency'. We need to have high expectations of pupils and teachers to ensure the best experience and outcomes in education, not only in what they learn but also in how they learn.

At a time of great change in education, we believe that it is important to reassert our commitment to core values through this book. Mutuality is achieved via collaboration and cooperation between pupils and their teachers, as well as between teachers. Through this approach, we believe that teachers and pupils will define and realise a 'good education' for pupils and teachers. This is a problematic and uncertain notion, but at the heart of education are dialogue, debate and the development of understanding at all stages of learning.

Ultimately, we believe that these principles will lead to the development of caring, skilled but engaged citizens in the school community. Long-term aims of education should not justify short-term deficits and inhumanity in the school learning experience, for pupils or their teachers. The journey towards a 'good education' for pupils and teachers is as important as the destination of lifelong educational skills, values and attitudes.

Mutuality between pupils and teachers

The mutuality principle in education explains the relationship between pupils and teachers as learners in school. Whilst the principal focus of the teacher is to ensure good progress and outcomes for pupils, in a good education they seek to do this within a positive classroom climate that encourages a constructive but challenging experience. As we have seen in previous chapters, the best professional development for teachers is located in disciplined enquiry, located in the authentic classroom. A good teacher education therefore explores the very learning that is the focus of their teaching. Even where there are experiences and challenges outside of the school, learning for children and adults is frequently a shared experience. At a simple level, the teacher experience is naturally wrapped up in the learning experience of the classroom. Motivated learners are more likely to promote motivated teaching and vice versa. Of course, the first responsibility for engaging lessons lies with the teacher, but, if we see self-regulated and self-directed learning as an aim, then pupils have a distinct and primary responsibility for their learning. With freedom for learning comes responsibility.

In this book, we have emphasised the need for good behaviour in the classroom. Generally accepted is the idea that this comes best from developing self-discipline in the learner. Not only do other learners deserve to be able to learn in class, but the teacher also has a reasonable right to be able to teach. Mutuality here extends between pupils and teachers, but also between pupils. Whilst individual pupils develop knowledge, the class as a collective is more or less effective, based on the ethos of the class, which reasonably allows others to engage with a teacher and learn more effectively. This is not to say that the teacher or pupil should resort to blaming one or the other if learning outcomes are not achieved. The mutuality principle suggests that responsibility for learning is shared between pupils and teachers. Likewise, where learners struggle to make expected progress because of a disability or learning difficulty, it is the responsibility of the teacher to act to ensure that a degree of learning support is put in place so that the learner can be scaffolded. Eventually, inclusion of all learners in this way provides a way for them all to achieve their potential. According to models of special education and disability, this is a pragmatic approach, recognising that there can be both internal (for instance, affective, neurological and cognitive) and external (social and organisational) barriers to learning. Unacceptable, though, is the artificial limitation of a child with special educational needs or disabilities (SEND) on the basis of low teacher expectations and a determination of too high a level of support, which develops learned helplessness in the pupil (Elliot and Dweck, 2013).

In this final chapter, we also make a case for a certain style of leadership to enable mutuality. Mutuality exists between teacher and pupils, pupils and pupils, but also between teachers and teachers. Specifically, teacher leaders must work with their staff in the spirit of mutuality to provide opportunities for engagement, motivation and empowerment. This book does not particularly focus on school leadership, but concepts such as distributed leadership and the servant–leader relationship are at the centre of mutuality between teachers and school leaders. Greenleaf's (2002) articulation of servant leadership could equally be applied in relation to the pupil and teacher role. Whilst the teacher certainly is a leader in class, effective classroom leaders achieve success less through the application of control, but more so through the empowering of learners. Likewise, accounts of leadership successes follow a familiar structure: a charismatic leader, often the chief executive officer (CEO) or school principal, takes over a struggling school, establishing new goals and expectations and challenging business as usual within the organisation. This leader creates new organisational routines and structures that with time transform the school's culture, contributing, in turn, to greater teacher satisfaction, higher teacher expectations for students and improved student achievement (Spillane, 2005). Again, we can see the spirit of mutuality in the distribution of leadership within the classroom. Classroom agency and empowerment are just as much about teachers carefully ensuring that their pupils have a sense of responsibility and ownership in the class. This means teachers developing effective ways of sharing control and ownership of learning with pupils.

Towards a better education for teachers and pupils

As has been seen in the work of Deci and Ryan (2008), the distinction between intrinsic or internal and extrinsic or external motivation is a false dichotomy. Whilst children may or may not enjoy listening to or playing classical music for the sheer joy of it, it is quite possible that engagement and motivation can shift, so that later in childhood, or even in adulthood, the joy of music becomes innate and an interest in itself. Many of us remember practising our musical scales, painfully at first, because this was required for our music exams; but later, as this enabled us to play more fluently, confidently and accurately, playing music became a pleasure in itself. Motivation for music has passed from an external to an internal locus. Playing music under sufferance and for external reward has passed to an intrinsically rewarding pursuit. Echoing the latest developments in activity theory (Engeström, 2001), internalisation is the process by which learners construct their cognitive understanding of the world, but it is also the process by which they develop engagement and motivation for learning.

Although we might all have different interests and motivations in life, as teachers we must recognise our responsibility to work on engaging pupils. The curriculum, therefore, goes beyond coverage of the statutory requirements of knowledge and skills to consider how we will plan to develop intrinsic motivation for a subject. A really good example here is the concern many schools have in relation to the standards of reading in boys, especially once they join secondary schools. We would not deny the importance of knowledge and skills in the decoding and comprehension process. After all, reading is not motivating if you cannot read. But schools and teachers must take responsibility to choose the subject matter and plan for sequences of learning that will inspire and engage pupils. For boys in reading, this might be in the choice of fiction and non-fiction texts that inspire them to enter a world of imagination, which they did not think was available to them. Teacher education should therefore help pre-service and qualified teachers to understand the process by which motivational patterns are internalised. By doing so, teachers will be able to engage pupils more, whilst almost certainly raising standards. No one who is disengaged in school is likely to do well. This includes teachers as well as pupils.

Teacher motivation and engagement through a process of internalisation are less well-explored, but no less important to the success of a school. Accountability through inspection in English schools is an area that cannot be dismissed. This impacts on engagement, motivation and empowerment of teachers. Jones and Tymms (2014) demonstrated that the key mechanisms that underpin Ofsted's promotion of school improvement are the setting of standards, giving feedback, the use of sanctions and rewards, the collection of information on schools, and public accountability. This has all the hallmarks of external regulation, rather than a school and education system that aspires to self-improvement and self-regulation. Cooper and Clyde (2014) state that despite the expense and frequency of inspection, most participants struggle to find benefit in terms of their own and students learning. Furthermore, marking, interaction with students, research and CPD lose out to the demands of inspection, impacting negatively on the student and staff experience. The research concludes that an atmosphere of fear inhibits learning and motivation, creating continuing after-effects including disillusionment, pressure, weariness, fear of redundancy and an urge to exit the profession, regardless of the grade received, which has profound implications for policy. Altrichter and Kemethofer (2015) explore the role of 'accountability pressure' as an element for understanding the operation of inspection systems using online survey data from over 2300 head teachers in seven European countries. The results indicate that heads who feel more 'accountability pressure' are more attentive to the quality expectations communicated by inspections, more sensitive to stakeholders' reactions to inspection results and more active with respect to improvement activities. However, the number of unintended consequences is increasing with pressure. Inspection systems in different countries are seen by school leaders as applying differential degrees of 'accountability pressure', which is reflected in system-specific amounts of improvement activities.

Despite the attempts to develop a self-improving system, it is clear that school inspection by Ofsted has a particular hold on teachers' engagement in schools. It would be unrealistic to expect any school system not to have a level of accountability, given the relatively high levels of public funding and high importance for the social, economic and cultural health of the nation. What we need is the right kind of accountability to lead to the right kind of engagement, motivation and empowerment of pupils and their teachers. It is beyond this book to suggest a new national inspection framework; however, we reiterate that a good model of accountability must lead to a good education. We emphasise a 'good education' of both pupils and their teachers. We believe that a good model of school accountability should emphasise the following factors:

Integrity: Do teaching and learning develop educationally sound processes and outcomes that are built on morally and professionally defensible foundations?

Agency: Do pupils and teachers take ownership and control of the learning process in school to ensure that learners are able to take responsibility and develop independence in their learning?

Validity: Do teaching and learning develop educationally justifiable approaches that are located in a broad evidence base?

Mutuality: Do teachers, pupils and school leaders share educational experiences, aims and outcomes that recognise the relationship between learning and teaching outcomes for both pupils and the professional development and growth of teachers?

Equity: How does the teacher and school ensure that high-quality learning is valued as a right for both pupils and teachers?

A good review of a good education should be a constant process carried out by all members of the school community: learners, teachers, administrators, parents, the wider community such as employers and, of course, external reviewers. If anything, the learners are in a privileged position and should be empowered to have a strong voice in any review process. We do not deny the role of an external consultant or expert in providing some objective qualitative and quantitative feedback to a school. But when this sometimes idiosyncratic voice becomes all powerful, it can exert an undue and distorting experience on the quality of learning outcomes and experiences for both pupils and teachers. In fact, Altrichter and Kemethofer (2015), quoted above, set those schools that are more at risk of adverse feedback and a bad inspection as being particularly sensitive to 'accountability pressure'. Naturally, a high-stakes accountability and testing system tends to lead to a focus on those criteria by which schools are judged accountable. Whilst on one measure inspection certainly leads to improvements in those areas that are the intended focus, there are unintended consequences of such an accountability model. In England, this has led to a narrowing of the curriculum, and many would argue that the 'accountability pressure' has been a factor in attrition rates in new and early career teachers (Cooper and Clyde, 2014). We need a proper national discussion in England about the best model for accountability in schools.

A better teacher education, a better schooling

Depending on where you live in the world, you might feel rather optimistic or pessimistic about the future of teacher education and schools. A hundred years from now, we doubt that education will look like it does currently. The curriculum will change, fashions and styles of teaching and learning will evolve. Some will come from educational experts, some from politicians (political educationalists and educational politicians). But we feel that there are some immutable universals in the best models of a good education. These principles of a good education are outlined below:

- A good education needs good learners.
- Pupils and their teachers are learners in school.
- A good education is a cognitive, social, emotional, moral and physical construct and experience.
- A good education is constructed by teachers and pupils and mediated through teachers and pupils.
- A good education is important for the present and the future: it is valuable in itself for the present, but it also helps to prepare the child for the current and future society.
- Education is a touchstone of society: how we treat children and adults and how much we encourage motivation, engagement and empowerment all says something about how we treat our citizens.
- Moving to a twenty-first- and twenty-second-century economy and society, uncertainty and therefore the need for flexibility, self-reflection, self-regulation and the ability to self-manage become even more important. An educational sector built on compliance, control and disempowerment just will not do for the economy and the future of the country.
- A good education must move beyond the self to develop learners' ability to become interdependent: reflection, regulation and management between and by individuals for the greater benefit of others and society in general should be an aim. This recognises the greater responsibility that individuals have, but it is different from compliance and ignorance of an educational system built on strong values. In fact, it is exactly the opposite.

We argue for a focus on a good education for both pupils and teachers rather than schooling for compliance. Teachers have the right to a good preparation and ongoing development for their roles. Having the time to make sense of evidence-based approaches to teaching and the application of educational principles is important for their own pupils, classrooms and schools. However, teachers also have a responsibility to their profession. Teachers should be public intellectuals, whether they are teaching 5-year-olds at a nursery school or 50-year-olds on a university doctoral programme. This means that they should have a strong voice as individuals, which must be built from their initial training programme on strong values, principles, and an ongoing and developing understanding of their metier. Educational issues are always challenging, but teachers should be able to articulate which are the best ways forward and why. This requires confidence.

Confidence comes from investment in people. Ultimately, we believe in people and their potential. We believe that trust in people is important. We believe that trust in teachers and learners comes from treating them decently, with integrity and with humanity:

When learners are empowered, they are motivated.

When learners are motivated, they are engaged.

When teachers are inspired, they inspire their learners.

When learners are inspired, there are no limits.

Chapter summary

- Values and humanity are at the centre of our approach to education – for both teachers and their pupils.
- High standards of learning should be expected of all learners.
- 'Flow' in the classroom is as much about the timeless experience of engagement in learning as it is about the fluid nature of learning and control over learning by the pupil and the teacher. A high-quality classroom experience is empowering for both pupils and teachers.
- Agency or the degree of control over the learning process is an important psychological as well as political reality. We argue that both pupils and their teachers must demonstrate 'agentive' learning both in the classroom and in their development as a teacher.
- The best professional development for teachers is located in disciplined enquiry, located in the authentic classroom. A good teacher education, therefore, explores the very learning that is the focus of their teaching.
- Mutuality exists between teacher and pupils, pupils and pupils, but also between teachers and teachers. Specifically, teacher leaders must work with their staff in the spirit of mutuality to provide opportunities for engagement, motivation and empowerment.
- Echoing the latest developments in activity theory (Engeström, 2001), internalisation is the process by which learners construct their cognitive understanding of the world, but it is also the process by which they develop engagement and motivation for learning.
- Teacher motivation and engagement through a process of internalisation are less well explored, but no less important to the success of a school. Accountability through inspection in English schools is an area that cannot be dismissed. This impacts on engagement, motivation and the empowerment of teachers.

- Whilst on one measure inspection certainly leads to improvements in those areas that are the intended focus, there are unintended consequences of such an accountability model. In England this has led to a narrowing of the curriculum, and many would argue that the 'accountability pressure' has been a factor in attrition rates in new and early career teachers (Cooper and Clyde, 2014).
- Teachers should be public intellectuals, whether they are teaching 5-year-olds at a nursery school or 50-year-olds on a university doctoral programme.
- This means that they should have a strong voice as individuals, which must be built from their initial training programme on strong values, principles, and an ongoing and developing understanding of their metier.
- Educational issues are always challenging, but teachers should be able to articulate which are the best ways forward and why. This requires confidence.

Further reading

Altrichter, H. and Kemethofer, D. (2015) 'Does accountability pressure through school inspections promote school improvement?', *School Effectiveness and School Improvement*, 26 (1): 32–56.
This article explains the concept of accountability in schools and how this links to school improvement. It is not a simple and uncomplicated relationship. There is an argument that different forms of accountability have a more or less negative impact on the wider experiences of learning in school.

Rogers, C.R. (1963a) 'The concept of the fully functioning person', *Psychotherapy: Theory, Research & Practice*, 7 (1): 17–26.
The author's seminal text on the full-functioning person. This is a very imprtant concept. Written in the 1960s, it provides a great insight into the humanistic view of the learner.

Schunk, D.H., Meece, J.R. and Pintrich, P.R. (2012) *Motivation in Education: Theory, Research, and Applications*. Harlow: Pearson Higher Education.
Another seminal text, here explaining the link between motivation, learning and self-regulation.

Bibliography

Altrichter, H. and Kemethofer, D. (2015) 'Does accountability pressure through school inspections promote school improvement?', *School Effectiveness and School Improvement*, 26: 32–56.

Cooper, B. and Clyde, H. (2014) '*An inspector palls: The problematic impact of OFSTED on learning and affect in teacher education and implications for policy*', British Educational Research Association (BERA) Annual Conference, 23–24 September, Institute of Education, London.

Csikszentmihalyi, M. (1990) 'The domain of creativity', in M.A. Runco and R.S. Albert (eds), *Theories of Creativity*. Newbury Park, CA: Sage.

Deci, E.L. and Ryan, R.M. (2008) 'Facilitating optimal motivation and psychological well-being across life's domains', *Canadian Psychology*, 49 (1): 14–23.

Elliot, A.J. and Dweck, C.S. (2013) *Handbook of Competence and Motivation*. New York: Guilford Press.

Engeström, Y. (2001) 'Expansive learning at work: Toward an activity theoretical reconceptualization', *Journal of Education and Work*, 14 (1): 133–56.

Greenleaf, R.K. (2002) *Servant Leadership: A Journey into the Nature of Legitimate Power and Greatness*. Mahwah, NJ: Paulist Press.

Jones, K. and Tymms, P. (2014) 'Ofsted's role in promoting school improvement: The mechanisms of the school inspection system in England', *Oxford Review of Education*, 40 (3): 315–30.

Rogers, C.R. (1963a) 'The concept of the fully functioning person', *Psychotherapy: Theory, Research & Practice*, 7 (1): 17–26.

Rogers, C.R. (1963b) 'Toward a science of the person', *Journal of Humanistic Psychology*, 3 (2): 72–92.

Schunk, D.H., Meece, J.R. and Pintrich, P.R. (2012) *Motivation in Education: Theory, Research, and Applications*. Harlow: Pearson Higher Education.

Spillane, J.P. (2005) 'Distributed leadership', *Educational Forum*, 69 (2): 143–50.

Zee, M. and Koomen, H.M. (2016) 'Teacher self-efficacy and its effects on classroom processes, student academic adjustment, and teacher well-being: A synthesis of 40 years of research', *Review of Educational Research*, 86 (4): 981–1015.

INDEX